UNIQUE EATS AND EATERIES

OF

THE PEOPLE AND STORIES BEHIND THE FOOD

REEDY PRESS

Copyright © 2024 by Reedy Press, LLC
Reedy Press
PO Box 5131
St. Louis, MO 63139, USA
www.reedypress.com

Library of Congress Control Number: 2024930283

ISBN: 9781681065311

Design by Jill Halpin

Cover photo credits, clockwise from top: Municipal Fish Market, courtesy of Bien Stephenson, Wikimedia Commons; Pineapple and Pearls, courtesy of Scott Suchman; Lapis, courtesy of Lapis; Elizabeth's Gone Raw, courtesy of Elizabeth's Gone Raw; L'Auberge Chez François, courtesy of James Diedrich.

Back cover photo credits: see credits for these photos on their interior pages.

Interior photos by author unless otherwise noted.

Title page photo credits, from top left to right:
Maydān, Rey Lopez; Elcielo, Andrea Grieco; Pineapple & Pearls, Scott Suchman; Xiquet, Sarah Matista; Elizabeth's Gone Raw; Jônt; Causa, Rey Lopez; Anafre, Scott Suchman; Masseria, Scott Suchman; Zaytinya, Rey Lopez; Astro Doughnuts & Fried Chicken, Scott Suchman; Laos in Town, Rey Lopez.

Printed in the United States of America
24 25 26 27 28   5 4 3 2 1

UNIQUE EATS AND EATERIES

OF

THE PEOPLE AND STORIES BEHIND THE FOOD

JOANN HILL

Torched Oysters at Bronze.
Photo courtesy of Alex Clirror.

BRONZE

DEDICATION

To my parents, who instilled upon us that food is as much a love language as it is a superpower. From lovingly prepared meals to nightly gatherings around the table, you showed us the pure joy and magic of food.

Dessert is served at Agora.
Photo courtesy of Shab & Coop.

CONTENTS

Find sipsational cocktails at Shababi's pop-up events.
Photo courtesy of Farrah Skeiky

ACKNOWLEDGMENTS

My love affair with food began at a very young age. Family dinners were often characterized by heaping plates of pasta tossed with my mom's homemade tomato sauce, plates brimming with vegetables grown in our garden, bowls of oil-cured olives, hunks of provolone, tins of anchovies, and fresh figs picked from my dad's fig tree. Food has always been the way my family shows love and the primary way we pay tribute to our Sicilian heritage. There were plenty of times as a kid when I longed for the foods my friends had at their houses that were all but forbidden in mine (what I would have given for a can of SpaghettiOs!). Today, of course, I am grateful that my parents emphasized the importance of home-cooked meals and fresh ingredients. Mom and Dad, for this, and much more, thank you.

To the illustrious chefs, bakers, beverage experts, restaurateurs, chocolatiers, market owners, barbecue and gelato masters, and hospitality specialists, this book would not be possible without you. Thank you for sharing your stories, filling our bellies, connecting our communities, and contributing to the vibrancy of our capital city. It has been an absolute honor to showcase you and your immense talents.

To the team at Reedy Press, thank you for your continuous guidance and entrusting me with such a meaningful project. Three books down with no plans of stopping any time soon! So incredibly grateful to be on this wild ride with you!

To my husband: my person, my purpose, and my ultimate taste tester. There's no one in the world I would rather indulge in double, sometimes triple, dinners with on Sundays (all in the name of research, of course). You are the light that illuminates my life and the spark that ignites my soul. I love you so very much.

INTRODUCTION

What makes an eatery unique? Its history? Its place and significance within a region? The individuals behind it and their inspiring life stories? As I interviewed and became acquainted with dozens of chefs, bakers, restaurateurs, and beverage experts across the DC area, it became abundantly clear that uniqueness lies in every one of these aspects. From iconic institutions like Ben's Chili Bowl and the Municipal Fish Market to lesser-known gems like Balangay and Amore Eats, this book is a wide-sweeping collection of the diverse eateries and individuals that help define our capital city.

Despite the many differences of the people behind the DC area's food and drink cultures, I was fascinated by how similar their stories were. Whether I was talking with a classically trained chef or someone who learned to cook and bake alongside their grandmother, nearly every single individual credited three sources of inspiration: family, tradition, and heritage. Regardless of their culinary path, their passion was inevitably birthed from a place of love, reverence, and resolve.

From fleeing war-torn countries to scraping together life savings to open the food truck or bakery of their dreams, these stories are living testaments to the underlying commitment, grit, and sacrifices that often go unnoticed in DC's dynamic dining scene.

As you bite into this book, my hope is that you will be inspired to occasionally stray from your trusted local haunts and venture beyond familiar flavors and foods. Head to lesser-visited neighborhoods like Anacostia to enjoy a plate piled high with jollof rice at Open Crumb followed by a visit to Lamond Riggs to wash down a cold pint of saison at Hellbender Brewing Company. Fall in love with the flavors of Egypt as you dig into a comforting bowl of koshary at Fava Pot and satisfy your sweet tooth with a luscious assortment of

Azerbaijan pastries like pakhlava and shorgoghal at Sharbat bakery and café. Indulge in an extravagant multicourse meal at a Michelin-starred restaurant like Jônt, savor pupusas on a Mount Pleasant corner, and meander through aisles of sweet and savory specialties at A. Litteri and Yekta Persian Market & Kabob Counter, two of the oldest markets in the region. Sip on a Middle Eastern cocktail at the Green Zone, sink your teeth into a Chesapeake cheesesteak at FishScale, wrap your hands around a steaming mug of tea at Teaism, and discover divinity in a cup as you devour Puddin's famous brown butter bourbon bread puddin'.

My greater hope is that you will also become more acquainted with the talented individuals who nourish our city: the people who work 16-hour days in the pursuit of satisfying our cravings and tantalizing our taste buds; those who honor their roots and share their cultures and upbringings in every single morsel and drop that emerges from their ovens, barrels, and smoke pits; the ones we turn to when we yearn for a delicious meal, gather with loved ones, celebrate birthdays and graduations, and long for soothing tastes of home.

Unique Eats and Eateries of Washington, DC showcases the region's wealth of gastronomic diversity, where heritage and history shape the city's thriving culinary landscape, and its vast cultural richness is brilliantly baked into every bite.

Brioche Stuffed Chicken at Bresca.
Photo courtesy of Bresca

UNIQUE EATS AND EATERIES

OF

WASHINGTON, DC

FAVA POT

Eat like an Egyptian

When in doubt, look for the beauty and hope around you; you never know where it may lead. Just ask Dina Daniel, chef and founder of Fava Pot, a DMV Egyptian food-truck-turned-restaurant sensation.

Dina moved to DC in 2004, and while she left her beloved birthplace, its rich customs and unyielding spirit remained in her heart. Noticing that Egyptian cuisine was sorely lacking in the area, she set out to bring her country's food and culture to DC. At 44, and against the advice of many, Dina purchased a truck and opened Fava Pot food truck in Tysons Corner. While she had no formal cooking experience, her love for her home stoked a fire in her, inspiring her to do whatever it took to turn her dream into a reality. Dina was on her own for the first three months, working 16-hour days often in harsh winter weather. She gave out samples of kofta and falafel to nearby offices in hopes of attracting customers and exposing people to the food of her homeland.

Missing loved ones and facing seemingly insurmountable obstacles soon began to take a toll. As Dina explains, home cooking is the core of Egyptian cuisine; meals are cooked to order with only the freshest of ingredients. Fava Pot's signature falafel are prepared from scratch, and their fava beans are slow cooked for 12 hours in exotic spices. Preserving the authenticity of Egyptian food is imperative to Dina, resulting in long hours of cooking and same-day market trips. She began to question if this was the right path for her. Just as she had convinced herself to abandon her dream, one morning Dina noticed a tulip blooming outside of her window. Marveling at its beauty and the undeniable signal of hope it represented, she recognized the sign that she needed to continue on her journey.

Left: Fava Pot favorites Kothary and falafel. *Center:* Teamwork makes the dream work for Dina Daniel (left) and Stephen Samuels (right). *Right:* There's something delicious for everyone at Fava Pot. Photos courtesy of Fava Pot.

Over a decade after opening her food truck, Dina owns two award-winning restaurants and a food cart in Tysons Corner Mall. She is grateful to her devoted team and honors her upbringing by encouraging guests to dine in a communal setting rather than eating at home in isolation.

As I sit across from Dina, devouring a comforting bowl of koshary, a diner stops by and politely shares that the food here is the closest that he's ever had to his mother's cooking. He graciously thanks Dina for these nourishing flavors of home. A wide smile spreads across Dina's face, and I know she's thinking, *That's exactly why I'm here.*

1817 M St. NW, 202-492-6919
7393 D Lee Hwy., Falls Church, VA, 202-492-6919
www.favapot.com

In addition to serving lunch and dinner, Fava Pot's Falls Church location also serves breakfast, including Egyptian-style breakfast sandwiches, omelets, and Fetter Meshaltet, an Egyptian flaky pastry served with honey and Egyptian feta cheese.

RAMEN ROYALTY

Katsuya Fukushima brings soul-satisfying ramen and so much more to DC's culinary landscape

Ramen has taken the world by storm, with DC ravenously following suit. The magical combination of noodles bathed in soulful stocks steeped in nori and spices elicits a gratifying sense of comfort. When it comes to slurping, DC has an embarrassment of riches, with Chef Katsuya Fukushima offering some of the city's very best.

A "military brat" of a Japanese-Hawaiian father, Katsuya moved to the US at four years old. He attended the University of Maryland but ultimately lost his scholarship, succumbing to the newfound freedom of college. He worked several jobs to pay for tuition, but it was a week-long cooking stint that would ultimately seal his fate. Katsuya enrolled in culinary school and landed an internship at Vidalia, one of DC's most prestigious restaurants. Grueling work conditions caused him to question his path, but his hunger for knowledge forced him to persevere. He worked tirelessly at restaurants across DC, learning from the likes of renowned chefs Ann Cashion and José Andrés. His cooking career was catapulted by a 15-year tenure with Andrés, during which he opened and operated dozens of Andrés's restaurants, including DC's highly lauded minibar.

Katsuya's career took another leap in 2013 when he met Yama Jewayni and Daisuke Utagawa. They invited him to join them in opening a ramen shop. With that, a burgeoning partnership—along with Daikaya, their acclaimed flagship restaurant of ramen and izakaya—was born. Following the resounding success of Daikaya, Bantam King—a fried chicken and ramen joint—and Haikan—a Sapporo-style ramen restaurant, opened in 2016.

Left: Daikaya's Sapporo-style ramen. Photo courtesy of Daikaya. *Center:* Owner and chef Fukushima being playful at Daikaya Ramen Shop. Photo courtesy of Vina Sananikone. *Right:* Crab rangoons, with Old Bay and jalapeño marmalade. Photo courtesy of Haikan.

Katsuya and his team go to great lengths to procure high-quality ingredients. Their noodles come from Sapporo's Nishiyama Seimen Co., where crystal-clear water cascades down neighboring mountains collecting countless minerals along the way, resulting in an unparalleled noodle. The team spent four days testing noodles, ultimately choosing a thicker, wavy-style noodle that grips the flavor of their delicate chintan broth. Noodles arrive frozen and are stored and then aged outside for a week, producing a deeper flavor, smell, and texture.

Katsuya's latest venture, Tonari, highlights wafu (Japanese style) Italian cuisine, which was popularized during the American occupation of Japan after World War II. Donning a Pizza Hut fleece, Katsuya shared his affinity for the popular chain along with Italian food. Tonari honors Katsuya's heritage with a touch of playfulness, fusing Japanese and Italian flavors. Mouthwatering dishes like mentaiko-and-corn pizza and Uni Uni Unico pasta help round out its ingenious menu.

Bantam King
501 G St. NW, 202-733-2612
bantamking.com

Daikaya
705 6th St. NW, 202-589-1600
daikaya.com

Haikan
805 V St. NW, 202-299-1000
haikandc.com

Tonari
707 6th St. NW, 202-289-8900
www.tonaridc.com

BAKED BY YÆL

Yael Krigman bakes everyone happy

What happens when a DC attorney embarks upon a failed bagel mission and decides to bake matters into her own hands? She whips up her own batch of baked beauties, follows her heart, and decides to change her career. And so, Yael Krigman, a self-proclaimed recovering attorney, entered DC's bakery scene, and our carb-loving bellies have been rejoicing ever since.

Yael began baking regularly. Each Monday she hand-delivered treats to her colleagues, sparking questions like, "Is it Monday yet?" and "When are you going to open up a bakery?" For a year, Yael grinded her way through two demanding careers, but it was an email by shuttered media megastar Daily Candy that determined Yael's fate. They put Yael and her bagels on the map when they declared her bagels as the best they'd ever had. The media outlet may no longer be with us, but we're eternally thankful that Baked by Yael is.

Yael launched a Kickstarter campaign in 2013 to help open DC's first cakepoppery. Six hundred sixty-nine backers pitched in to raise an astounding $75,000. Many were friends and former colleagues, while others were strangers. One of those generous strangers in particular stood out, so much so that Yael decided to marry him.

The decision to designate Baked by Yael as nut-free has had a profound effect on many customers, some embracing her in tears as they emotionally share that this is the first time their children felt safe inside a bakery. She doesn't want allergens or special diets to deprive anyone of life's simple pleasures. Many confections are vegan and gluten-free, including the black-and-white cookies and hamantaschen, a three-cornered cookie filled with apricot or raspberry. The bakery also holds two kosher certifications.

Left: Eyes-rolling-in-the-back-of-your-head-worthy challah. *Center:* Bagel beauties. Photos courtesy of Yael Krigman. *Right:* Owner and baker extraordinaire Yael Krigman. Photo courtesy of Joseph Gruber.

Yael knows she's nailed a recipe when her eyes roll to the back of her head. She was reluctant to serve challah, a Jewish bread that's personal to many who associate the braided loaf with their grandmother's and special occasions. After numerous attempts, her eyes started to roll, and that's when she knew her challah deserved a permanent spot at her bakery.

Baked by Yael has earned tremendous success and notoriety, including its challah making its theatrical debut in the National Theater's production of *Fiddler on the Roof*. And while Yael no longer hand-delivers treats to her colleagues on Mondays, the firm she left in 2012 continues to order 100 *Wednesday* treats to this day, a testament to her extraordinary products and remarkable character.

Multiple locations
Main Bakery: 3000 Connecticut Ave. NW, 202-234-9235
bakedbyyael.com

The "small and mighty" bakery ships nationwide. Visit Baked by Yael's website for their full catalog of cake pops, pastries, sandwiches, challah, and more. Custom treats, cookies, and cake pops are available upon request. Contact them for a taste of joy and sweetness at your next corporate or smaller catering event, birthday, b'nai mitzvahs, weddings, and more.

A. LITTERI

Selling Italian products and wine since 1926

It's easy to miss A. Litteri's Italian market amid the posh and revitalized Union Market/NoMa neighborhood. Minus the Italian-flag-painted door, the unassuming exterior blends into its neighboring warehouse facades, a modest lot among a sea of stylish storefronts. Owner Max Evans wouldn't want it any other way. Preserving its history is all part of the work involved in honoring its humble beginnings.

The oldest Italian market in DC, A. Litteri remained in the Litteri family for three generations. Eventually, ownership changed hands and Ken Nankervis ran the market until his passing in 2019. Life came full circle for Max Evans, A. Litteri's former wine distributor, when he was asked to help run the market during Ken's illness. Max bought the market in 2019, causing the generations of families who have frequented the market for nearly a century to breathe a sigh of relief.

An Italian market akin to those in Philadelphia and Manhattan, A. Litteri is a rarity in the DMV. Shoppers are greeted by a cornucopia of Italian products like pastas, vinegars, and olive oils. Italian cookies are brought in from Brooklyn while sodas and candies are sourced from New Jersey. Its repertoire of cheeses like gorgonzola and provolone, and meats like salami and house-made sausages, would make any Italian grandmother swoon.

Head back to the deli counter for a quintessential Italian sub. The classic—stuffed with genoa salami, capicola, mortadella, prosciuttini, and all the fixings—is a perennial favorite among customers.

And then there's the wine. So. Much. Wine. In 2017, the *Washington Post* proclaimed A. Litteri as one of the best places in the world to buy Italian wine outside of Italy. You'll find a vast

Top left: Italian cheeses and desserts. *Above left:* A beautiful bouquet of meats and cheeses. *Top right:* A. Litteri's quintessential Italian sub. *Above right:* Bottles are bountiful at A. Litteri. Photos courtesy of A. Litteri, Inc.

selection of varietals like Barolo and Barbera as well as rarer vintages like Grignolino from Piedmont. Max loves the "weird ones," like Erbaluce and Ribolla giallo, both white varieties, and equally loves recommending them to patrons. While chatting with Max and his counterpart, James Ellis, Max smiles as he recalls a customer on the hunt for three unusual wines: Allbana Secco, Pingnoletto, both from Emilia-Romagna, and Passerina from Abbruzzo. Of course, they had all three. This, among countless other reasons, is why so many continue to come back year after year. From the millennial who's new to the neighborhood to the family who has come in every Saturday for decades, A. Litteri is more than a DC institution; it's a place that feels like home.

517 Morse St. NE, 202-544-0183
alitteri.com

Order Italian subs, salads, pastas, and soups either at the deli counter or online. Catering menus are also available.

PUDDIN'

Divine comfort food

While most food-centric stories save the dessert section for the end, Puddin's famous Brown Butter Bourbon Bread Puddin' has earned the distinction of being first mentioned. Warm, buttery bourbon goodness soaked up by moist bread pudding might just be the impetus behind the saying, "Eat dessert first." This is soul-satisfying comfort food at its best. It's also owner Toyin Alli's "happiest accident," a one-off recipe mistake that produced a crowd-pleasing creation. The long-lasting result? Divinity spooned into a cup.

Toyin's love for cooking is influenced by her father's Nigerian heritage and her mother's Southern roots. While traveling through Louisiana she discovered the deep connection between West African cuisine and Southern fare, learning more about the history of enslaved cooks and their pivotal role in the birth of our country's cultural heritage. Enslaved cooks introduced Southern staples like okra and greens to create signature dishes like gumbo and étouffée. Growing up, Toyin's mom loved the gumbo at an eatery near their home because it reminded her of the gumbo she enjoyed with her family. Today, Toyin creates her own version of the family favorite while staying true to its origin, opting for a seafood base instead of a roux, and adding bursts of flavor with okra, smoked shrimp, and notes of sassafras.

Moving from California, Toyin was immediately captivated by DC's farmers market scene, spending countless hours exploring and dreaming of being a vendor. She began fueling her passion by catering events and luncheons, all while keeping her eye on the prize: landing a coveted space at Eastern Market. When her application was finally accepted, she devoted every waking moment to cooking

Left: Puddin's famous Brown Butter Bourbon Bread Puddin'. *Center:* Sink your teeth into a Shrimp Po'boy. *Right:* Beautiful bowls of comfort including red beans 'n rice and shrimp 'n grits. Photos courtesy of Puddin'.

comfort food, building her brand, and earning her reputation across the region.

Toyin upped the ante when she purchased a former ice-cream truck off Craigslist for $2,000. She painted the truck black and invested every dollar she had in fixing it up, replacing the engine, adding a refrigerator, and eventually adding signage. Toyin's investment has certainly paid off. Puddin's slick and shiny wheels have sent the DC area's taste buds on the mouthwatering ride of their lives.

Puddin' has grown considerably since its inception. Today, Toyin's divine Southern comfort food has attracted a devout following. Patrons queue up for Toyin's shrimp 'n grits, chicken 'n beef sausage gumbo, and of course, her establishment's namesake, her famed brown butter bourbon bread puddin'—a delectable treat as worthy of the story's conclusion as it is of its introduction.

Union Market: 1309 5th St. NE
dcpuddin.com

COMPASS ROSE | MAYDĀN

Rose Previte lights DC's food and wine scenes on fire

When Rose Previte discovered her first restaurant, Compass Rose, was featured in Lonely Planet, she knew she had arrived. Manifesting her ardor for food, travel, and the stories they generate, the avid traveler, restaurateur, and wine extraordinaire began the second act of her career (the first being in public policy) with blazing ferocity. DC's culinary scene has been on fire ever since.

During a three-year stint in Russia, Rose and her husband traveled to a staggering 30 countries. Their extensive travels had a profound effect on them, but it was their time in the Republic of Georgia that left the greatest impression. Rose cherishes the hospitality they received, as well as the fusion of dishes and flavors that she would someday re-create and share with others.

Rose drew upon her travels to open Compass Rose, a neighborhood gem influenced by the diverse street food she savored around the world. From its exotic atmosphere to its colorful menu, Compass Rose embodies the global pursuits that have helped shape her. Its dining concept, "armchair tasters," is based on the "armchair traveler" notion of being whisked away to foreign locales without leaving the comfort of home. Palates are treated to a world tour of dishes and wines hailing from destinations like Lebanon and Syria. Their acclaimed khachapuri, Georgian cheese bread accented by a runny egg, is so exceptional that it just might inspire you to book a ticket to Georgia to bask in all its culinary splendor.

In the Lebanese-Italian home where Rose grew up, family meals centered around open-fire cooking. She would later long for the traditional cooking methods of her youth. From this longing, Maydān

Top left: A Feast for Maydān's lamb shoulder is a feast for the senses. *Center:* Customize every dish to your liking with Maydān's captivating collection of condiments. Photos courtesy of Rey Lopez. *Bottom:* Inside Maydān's stunning interior. Photo courtesy of Dixie Vereen.

and its showstopping open hearth were born, a bold tribute to Rose's upbringing and culture. The roaring hearth serves as the centerpiece of the intimate space and its superlative plates. A sumptuous spread including luscious dips, kebabs, honey-drizzled halloumi, roasted vegetables, and pulled-from-the-oven pita bread transports diners to the bustling markets and communal tables sprinkled throughout the Middle East. Before opening Maydān, Rose and her team set out on a multi-week research trip throughout Morocco, Lebanon, Tunisia, Georgia, and Turkey, where they strayed from traditional methods of visiting restaurants and studying under chefs. Instead, they visited families' homes and learned under the guidance of grandmothers and other matriarchs.

Rose's "heart project," as she lovingly refers to her encore career, honors the diverse dishes that have influenced her, as well as the meanings and histories behind them.

Compass Rose
1346 T St. NW, 202-506-4765
compassrosedc.com

Maydān
1346 Florida Ave. NW, 202-370-3696
maydandc.com

AMORE EATS

Pumping out tasty Taiwanese cooking

Missing home and a love of her grandmother's cooking led Amore Eats co-owner Pei Hsieh to open a Taiwanese restaurant inside of a Rockville Exxon gas station. Pei was working in real estate when a friend asked her for help in scouting out a restaurant location. She came across the Exxon space and knew it was the perfect spot to open her first eatery. She enlisted the help of her longtime friend and real estate partner, Max Mo, and together they designed a space where they could re-create the familiar foods of their childhood while honoring the culinary history of their homeland.

Pei grew up surrounded by farmland and cooking alongside her grandmother, the woman who continues to inspire her to this day. Grocery stores were extremely scarce in the countryside; her family relied on the crops that they grew, particularly rice, the major food staple of the region. Living in the United States, Pei longed for her grandmother's cooking and the Hakka-inspired cuisine from her mother's side, often characterized by its sauce fermentation, pickled foods, and rice dishes. Pei and Mo developed a menu highlighting the specialties and sentimental flavors of their native home.

The menu at Amore Eats is categorized into three sections. Section A, "Xiao chi," or street food, features stinky tofu, popcorn chicken, and Pei's childhood favorite, Taiwan meatballs. Section B focuses on bento boxes. Taiwan was under Japanese colonial rule from 1895 to

> **Be on the lookout for special menu items, particularly seafood dishes highlighting the fresh catch brought in by Mo after his regular fishing trips.**

Left: Beef noodle soup. *Right:* Bento boxes. Photos courtesy of Amore Eats.

1945, and remnants of its influence still seep into Taiwan culture, including its food preparation and taste. Bento boxes are particularly popular in Pei's hometown region, Taitung, so much that there's a bento museum there! The bento boxes at Amore Eats include a myriad of medleys. Pei recommends trying the Taiwan sticky rice with eel, bacon, or dried baby shrimp. Lastly, the T and S sections highlight a range of soups, including their popular beef noodle soup, hot pots, and veggies, with a special focus on sweet cabbage, one of Pei's favorite vegetables to work with.

Working in a small kitchen can present some challenges. Pei shares that the staff must be very careful when moving around and equipment and ingredients are more limited than in a conventional kitchen. These obstacles, however, are quickly forgotten the moment you take a bite or slurp of Amore Eats' incredible cooking, proving that sometimes the most flavorful food can be found in the most unusual places.

1900 Rockville Pike, Rockville, MD
301-665-8999

PERUVIAN BROTHERS

Two brothers share their homeland passion and pride

La Cosecha is a marketplace mecca that leads visitors on a gastronomic whirlwind through Central and South America, Mexico, and the Caribbean without anyone having to board a plane. Peruvian Brothers, a fast-casual eatery showcasing the coastal flavors of Peru, helped pave the way as one of the market's premier merchants.

Peruvian Brothers Giuseppe and Mario Lanzone began their burgeoning business as a food truck. Born in Peru's oceanside district of La Punta, the siblings grew up working on boats and enjoying freshly caught seafood and produce of the region. They came to the US as teenagers, Giuseppe eventually becoming a two-time Olympic rower, and Mario honing in on his prowess in the kitchen. Following their individual successes, their mother

Top: Giuseppe and Mario Lanzone. *Above:* Pan con pollo. Photos courtesy of Peruvian Brothers.

suggested they open a food truck. Proving that moms typically know best, in 2013, their first truck went into operation. Their popularity led to several rewarding opportunities, including being a vendor at DC's Smithsonian Folklife Festival and cooking at the Embassy of Peru. Customer favorites include the chicharron sandwich and lomo saltado. Their vegetarian Triple sandwich honors the egg sandwich they ate growing up, and the cooling Clasico Ceviche will make you feel like you've stepped onto the shores of their beloved homeland.

Headquarters: 4592 Eisenhower Ave., Alexandria, VA, 703-625-6473

AREPA ZONE

Venezuelan tastes of nostalgia and connectivity

A chance meeting brought Arepa Zone cofounders Gabriela Febres and Ali Arellano together. The pair shared a love for their Venezuelan homeland and a talent for selling its products. Arepa Zone was born out of Antojitos de tu País, a sister company specializing in the distribution of Venezuelan foods. During her deliveries, Gabriela was often greeted with hugs and invitations to stay for coffee. Some of her customers would cry while embracing her, emotionally noting the foods that reminded them of home. Following a photo shoot marketing cachapas (Venezuelan corn pancakes), the duo were flooded with calls requesting restaurant reservations. They knew they had to seize this opportunity, and Arepa Zone's food truck hit the streets in 2014, becoming the region's first of its kind to serve Venezuelan arepas.

Arepa Zone filled a void not only for Gabriela's customers, but also for herself. She credits her family for keeping her tethered to her roots and affinity toward entrepreneurship, and her grandmother for her scratch-made baking. She laughs as she shares about her grandmother passing down "recipes" by saying, "add a little of this, and a little of that." Arepa Zone's popular polvorosas, cookies served at Gabriela's childhood birthday parties, are one of many of her grandmother's creations.

Top: Arepa de abellón
Above: Cachapa de queso de mano y pernil. Photos courtesy of Soho Studio.

Multiple locations
1121 14th St. NW, 202-900-2261
arepazone.com

INDIGO

A long-cherished dream and the unwavering support of a community

Ever since Nidhi and Dinesh Tandon moved here from Northern India, Nidhi dreamed of opening a restaurant. The self-taught home cook began taking her dishes to shops around Northern Virginia, where she would set up a table to sell her creations. Impressed by his wife's unrelenting work ethic, Dinesh applied to be an Eastern Market vendor. Their wait-list prompted him to look elsewhere, eventually securing a space outside of Union Station's North Hall. The couple worked 12-hour days in their five-by-five stall, cooking up Indian street food on their portable griddle. Patrons lined up for Nidhi's impeccable cooking, sometimes stretching to 60 customers deep. Their lease was cut short, but as fate would have it, an Eastern Market stall had become available. Within weeks, they joined the marketplace where they became a treasured fixture for the next two years.

One day, Dinesh stopped by a corner store and noticed that the store owner was boarding up the windows. Sensing an opportunity, Dinesh asked for the building's owner's phone number. The owner was familiar with their Eastern Market stall and agreed to meet with Dinesh that day. Shortly thereafter, Nidhi's dream of opening a restaurant finally came true. Indigo opened its doors in NoMa in September 2013.

Indigo's early days were built on the shoulders of a three-person team: Dinesh, Nidhi, and Dinesh's mother. They moved their family from their Arlington home to live above the restaurant, working around the clock to keep the eatery afloat. Dinesh remembers the beginning days of having only one dishwasher and no staff. Patrons would have to go back in the kitchen to collect their food orders. The neighborhood didn't seem to mind. Residents loved Indigo so

Left: Indigo lights up the NoMa neighborhood. *Center:* Husband-and-wife team Nidhi (right) and Dinesh (left) Tandon. *Right:* Indigo's one-of-a-kind ornate entrance. Photos courtesy of Indigo.

much that when they noticed long lines, many would come over, grab an apron, and help. When Dinesh applied for a liquor license and subsequently an outdoor bar, the community came out in droves, signing petitions and joining the march to town hall.

Over a decade later, Indigo remains a crown jewel of the community. Devoted diners continue to line up for Nidhi's delightful dishes like her butter chicken, reminiscent of the honey-flavored specialty she's cooked countless times for her children. It's hard not to smile as you enter the casual and eclectic eatery. Customer love notes adorning its cheerful walls serve as beautiful mementos of the lasting power of a tight-knit community and a long-cherished dream.

243 K St. NE, 202-544-4777
indigowdc.com

Peruse Indigo's rotating menu and long list of specials on the chalkboard inside. Dishes are derived from a collection of multigenerational recipes with a loving twist from Nidhi. Try comforting classics like spicy chicken masala, goat curry, creamy lentils, and indiriolls (bread rolls bundled with sizzled meats and vegetables).

2FIFTY BBQ

Hand-crafted, wood-smoked BBQ and the pursuit of the American dream

When Fernando González found himself in Austin, Texas, several weeks longer than expected due to an issue with his shipping company, he had no idea he'd be overtaken by its barbecue. Wanting to acquaint himself with the city, he began googling things to do and stumbled upon dozens of barbecue-focused walking tours. He became obsessed with the Hill Country specialty, often visiting two barbecue joints a day, including legendary spots like Franklin Barbecue, where pioneer Aaron Franklin graciously gave him a tour of his smokers. González was enamored by every aspect of the West Texas staple, including the hospitality surrounding it.

2fifty BBQ's immense success is the collective result of González and wife/partner Debby Portillo's tenacity coupled with a Peruvian lawyer's resourcefulness. The El Salvadoran couple managed to establish US residency (and later citizenship) during an anti-immigrant administration and successfully opened a restaurant during a pandemic. A third-generation restaurateur, Portillo is the mastermind behind operations, while González uses his training as a civil engineer to zero in on the science behind the cooking process. González smokes his meat without the assistance of electricity or gas. Not one for shortcuts, he subscribes to a hands-on traditional approach, believing that the painstaking measures taken to uphold its integrity is worth it. He doesn't stop there, however. González and his team are adamant about preserving its history and have made the conscious decision to partner with premier purveyors Creekstone and Snake River Farms, both known for their sustainable farming practices devoid of antibiotics and added hormones.

Left: BBQ master and owner Fernando González putting the finishing touches on pulled pork. Photo courtesy of Rey Lopez. *Right:* Sliced BBQ platter. Photo courtesy of Sam Portillo.

González uses two 1,000-gallon and one 500-gallon chambers to smoke 2fifty's meats. The establishment's name represents the optimal Fahrenheit temperature inside his smokers. Sink your teeth into melt-in-your-mouth smoked meats like American Wagyu brisket, a cut González worked tirelessly to perfect. While trimming the brisket, he distributes his signature scratch-made salt-and-pepper mixture evenly across its slabs. Other succulent cuts include tender beef ribs, luscious pulled pork, and whole smoked chicken. González and Portillo don't shy away from incorporating delicacies from their homeland, like pupusas, and their own take on traditional sides like coleslaw and sweet baked beans. Portillo's red beans are simmered with brisket trimmings, just the way her mother taught her.

2fifty BBQ is the realization of a dream, strong conviction, and unrelenting grit. It's proved to be a winning recipe for some of the best barbecue east of the Lone Star state.

414 K St. NW
4700 Riverdale Rd., Rivervale, MD
2fiftybbq.com

Enthusiasts can fulfill all their barbecue dreams by preordering, scheduling pickups, and dining at 2fifty's sit-down restaurant. Be on the lookout for their Wednesday specials, pork belly burnt ends and chicharrones (fried rib tips), and the pitmaster's newest creations.

MAKAN

Malaysian fare worthy of much more than a stopover

Chef James Wozniuk hasn't always been obsessed with food. Sure, family dinners were important, and he enjoyed eating pickled vegetables grown in his grandmother's garden, but it wasn't until his early 20s that he started seriously cooking. While he was staying with his grandmother, the nearby university offered two programs for him to choose from: automotive and culinary arts. Wozniuk chose the latter in hopes that cooking would be useful when traveling. Unbeknownst to him, this choice would lead to a lifelong passion and prolific career.

The impetus for Wozniuk's love affair with Malaysian food was a 15-hour layover in Kuala Lumpur. He spent his time talking to locals and street hawkers and sampling as many delicacies as he could. While the accomplished chef was no stranger to Asian cuisine, the flavors he sampled in Kuala Lumpur were like nothing he had ever tasted. From durian to wok-fried noodles, he was blown away by the cuisine. Although brief, his experience had a profound effect on him. From that day forward, Wozniuk decided to learn all he could about Malaysia's people, food, and culture.

Wozniuk returned to Malaysia on three subsequent trips, each time spending several months eating, observing, and studying the multiethnic aspects of its cuisine. Makan, meaning "to eat" in Malay, is the culmination of Wozniuk's extensive research, enthusiasm, tenacity, and undeniable talent. The chef's primary goal is to help introduce and promote Malaysian cuisine, which is often unrepresented in the US. He uses food as a vehicle to create authentic and meaningful experiences for his guests. Wozniuk dedicates months to testing recipes and is committed to upholding

Left: Makan's mouthwatering marvels. *Right:* Makan owner and chef James Wozniuk. Photos courtesy of Hypefoodies.

the integrity of the dishes. If he's unable to procure an ingredient or he feels a dish fails to represent the culture in any way, he abandons it. Wozniuk and his team work tirelessly to honor the history and flavors of every plate they serve. Makan's menu highlights the diversity and breadth of Malaysian fare, including street food, noodle soups and dishes, sambal, curries, and mixed rice.

One of Chef's most rewarding experiences has been cooking regularly for the Malaysian Embassy staff. In 2022, Wozniuk's stellar résumé was further amplified when he was invited to cook for the then–Malaysian Prime Minister Dato' Sri Ismail bin Yaakob and more than 100 guests.

3400 11th St. NW, 202-730-2295
Thirsty Crow (downstairs)
Spicebird (pickup or delivery from Makan's front door)
makanrestaurantdc.com | thirstycrowdc.com | spicebirddc.com

Head downstairs to the Thirsty Crow, Chef Wozniuk's neighborhood sports bar specializing in East Asian bites including satay, dan dan noodles, and spring rolls. In the mood for a roast chicken with all the fixin's? Order from Spicebird, Wozniuk's casual takeout joint serving Southeast Asian spice-rubbed chicken accompanied by a menagerie of sauces and sides.

ELIZABETH'S GONE RAW

Elevated vegan cuisine that's as refined as it is ravishing

Imagine a lobster roll changing your life. That's precisely what happened when El Salvadorian native Francisco Hernandéz tasted the New England delicacy for the first time. Nearly two decades later, the executive chef of Elizabeth's Gone Raw (EGR) can still taste the chunks of lobster and buttery toasted bun, captivated by its simple perfection. Two bites and $24 later, Francisco knew he wanted to experience more indelible tasting moments like that lobster roll, and that he wanted to create similar experiences for others.

The self-taught chef moved to DC seeking out seafood restaurants to hone his craft while simultaneously sampling more seafood specialties, this time without the $24 price tag. Francisco's hunger for learning and his work ethic landed him a job at Georgetown's Hook. He jokingly recalls that he couldn't believe that the restaurant was paying him; he would have gladly cooked for free. Each day he stayed hours after his shift, mesmerized by the energy of the kitchen and enthralled by the "superhero" staff that commanded the kitchen.

One day, a friend of Francisco's reached out with an opportunity to cook at EGR, a vegan, raw, and organic restaurant, a first of its kind in the metropolitan area. Francisco had zero experience working with vegan food; kitchen tools like dehydrators and low-temperature cooking methods were completely foreign to him. But he was no stranger to hard work and relished the challenge. Francisco fully immersed himself, experimenting with cooking at temperatures less than 112 degrees and concocting desserts absent of sugar, flour, and dairy. He incorporated ingredients like avocado and nuts when creating cheeses and dishes. He did have one stipulation for founder

24

Left: A gorgeous garden on a plate. *Center:* Raspberry done in two delectable ways. *Right:* Palette-able bites. Photos courtesy of Elizabeth's Gone Raw.

and owner Elizabeth Petty: he wanted to cook but didn't want the title of being the executive chef. Elizabeth assured him she would look for a head chef. Twelve years later, Francisco continues to lead the establishment, mentoring his team as he shares the techniques and over 2,500 plant-based recipes he's penned and mastered along the way.

Elizabeth founded EGR as a testament to the plant-based diet she adopted after surviving a battle with breast cancer. From the beginning, Elizabeth has been resolute in using natural and healthy ingredients in an imaginative and purposeful manner. Elizabeth and Francisco are far more than colleagues—they are family. Francisco's daughter refers to Elizabeth as "grandmother" and the humble chef affectionately describes her as "one of the best people he's ever met."

1341 L St. NW, 202-347-8349
elizabethsgoneraw.com

Elizabeth's Gone Raw is open three nights a week: Thursday, Friday, and Saturday evenings. Their six-course tasting menu changes every two months.

FRANKLY . . . PIZZA!

Let's be frank. This pizza is delicious.

Walking into Frankly . . . Pizza!, it's clear that you've stepped into someplace special. Yes, the pizza is heavenly, but this Kensington stalwart is much more than that. It's a place where values of family, humanity, and teamwork seep into every crevice and simplicity is celebrated. Staff members cajole with guests and blithely sing and dance while kneading dough and pouring beers. The utter joy that emanates from this neighborhood nook might almost make you forget why you came here in the first place. Almost.

Owner and self-proclaimed pizza lover Frank Linn grew up surrounded by homegrown food and home-cooked meals. Sit-down family dinners centered around their garden's vegetables, and the importance of fresh food, was instilled upon Frank.

Frank pored over culinary books, and although he was at times discouraged from pursuing a culinary career, that only made him more determined. He built a pizza oven in his backyard, spent years creating the perfect dough, and tweaked the sauce recipe that had been in his family for over 80 years. The tremendous support he received from family and friends inspired Frank to take his pizza on the road. After two years of carting around his mobile pizza oven to farmers markets and getting an overwhelmingly positive reception, Frank opened his dream restaurant, aptly named Frankly . . . Pizza! A decade later his pizza passion project continues to be a cherished favorite among neighbors and critics alike.

Frank describes his pizza as a bit unruly, just like the untamed crust he loved as a kid. The charred, bubbly crust is intentional, allowing for a hint of bitterness to balance out the sweetness of the sauce and the saltiness of melted cheese and house-made meats like sausage and meatballs. Each pizza that emerges from their oak-fired brick oven

Top left: Pizza sampler. *Above left:* Spinach pizza. *Top right:* Pesto pizza. Photos courtesy of Simo Ahmadi of Photography by Simo. *Above right:* Margherita pizza. Photo courtesy of Jeffrey Justiniano.

is intended to be a multisensory experience that invites diners to eat with their eyes, smell aromatic herbs, and taste a sublime symphony of gooey, crunchy, and nutty flavors. Years of experimenting in his backyard has paid dividends in his cozy restaurant kitchen. One key technique that distinguishes Frank's pizza is spraying the dough with oil to protect it from burning and to curb its bitterness.

The Hot Mess, Frank's signature pizza, is a mouthwatering mixture of mozzarella, pickled jalapeños, caramelized onions, bacon, Gruyère, and Romano. Frank describes the spinach white pizza as powerful, just like his personality, and the pepperoni is a favorite among kids and traditionalists.

10417 Armory Ave., Kensington, MD, 301-832-1065
franklypizza.com

Frank's pizzas are divided into two categories: red pies and white pies. Each pizza is a personal pizza, measuring about 12 inches. Gluten-free pizza is available by advance request for an additional fee and can be reserved on their website.

PINEAPPLE & PEARLS

You're invited to a party of epic proportions

Sometimes one experience can change the entire trajectory of your life. An afternoon with family friend Jonathan Krinn of 2941 exploring the restaurant's garden and kitchen was all Aaron Silverman needed to know that he wanted to be a chef. He graduated college a year early and enrolled in culinary school. After 10 years of building an impressive résumé that includes Momofuku in Manhattan and McCrady's in Charleston, Silverman returned home to begin planning his first restaurant, Rose's Luxury. Three years later, the Michelin-starred chef opened Pineapple & Pearls next door to equal fanfare.

When Pineapple & Pearls reopened on the heels of the pandemic, Silverman reimagined it as "fancy fun": a notion that incorporates haute cuisine while embracing familiarity and approachability. While Silverman felt they had previously bent the mold of fine dining, they hadn't broken it. Its transformation would not only break it but *smash* it, leaving the traditional fine-dining model behind and proving that elevated cuisine needn't be intimidating to be exceptional. As Chef Silverman explains, he and his team are in the business of making people happy. "THIS IS A PARTY. Every night. You just happen to get an amazing meal while you are here," its website declares.

If there was ever a time to raid your closet, this is it. Don your flashy sequin dress and dust off your snazzy velvet jacket; you've been invited

---

Because luxury shouldn't be limited to dining out! Rose's at Home offers unique and first-class dining experiences in the comfort of your home. Visit their website to learn more about available dinner parties, events, and monthly home dinner and wine memberships.

Left: A glimpse into Pineapple & Pearls's celebratory dining room. Photo courtesy of Anna Meyer. *Center:* Topping off dessert at Pineapple & Pearls. *Right:* Pineapple & Pearls's three-cheese ravioli. Photos courtesy of Scott Suchman.

to a party of epic proportions, and only your fancy-fun best will do. Guests are greeted with a handcrafted cocktail before being escorted to a bedazzled dining room accentuated by a canopy of balloons and luminous disco balls.

A lengthy tasting menu has been replaced by a shorter one, characterized by four substantial courses punctuated by a smattering of gifts. A pair of beggar's purses, arguably its most spellbinding course, features exquisite beet-and-saffron-colored crepes bursting with caviar and crème fraiche, topped with a gold leaf and more glorious caviar. These blissful bundles are designed to be picked up with your lips, another indication to abandon your inhibitions at the door. Expect showstopping courses like sinful soufflés, pillowy pastas, indulgent Japanese surf and turf, and a delectable take on the regional favorite "crab feast." Don't be surprised if your dreams that evening are dominated by pasta; Marco's gnocchi and "three cheese" ravioli are testaments to Silverman's favorite food. A parade of dreamy desserts including a trip to the pull-your-own buttered popcorn soft-serve machine crown off the extravagant affair.

Pineapple & Pearls
715 8th St. SE, 202-595-7375
pineappleandpearls.com

Rose's Luxury
717 8th St. SE, 202-742-3570
rosesluxury.com

THE SOLIS SIBLINGS

El Sol, Mezcalero, Mariscos 1133, Anafre, and the brother-and-sister team behind their culinary empire

Growing up in Mexico City, Alfredo Solis had a knack for being late for family meals. His mother made it abundantly clear: she wasn't running a restaurant, so if Solis wanted to eat, he'd have to cook for himself. Nearly 20 years have passed since Chef Solis arrived in DC, and Washingtonians have been applauding his tardiness (and his mother's tough love) ever since.

A few years after landing a dishwashing job in San Diego, Solis followed his cousin's advice and moved to DC. He worked two jobs, one including the defunct D.C. Coast, launching his culinary career with Passion Food Hospitality. He spent 15 years climbing the group's ladder, eventually earning the prestigious role of executive chef. Around 2007, Alfredo convinced his sister Jessica to leave her taqueria in Mexico and join him in Washington. She worked as a line cook, her impeccable cooking skills immediately earning recognition. As Alfredo proudly proclaims, "She cooks better than me."

The siblings shared a common goal: opening their own restaurant. They started a business out of Jessica's apartment, selling tacos and tortas to industry friends. After years of saving and working multiple jobs, they opened El Sol in 2016. Evoking the foods of their childhood, El Sol pays homage to Mexico City street food. Large glossy menu pages overflow with mouthwatering marvels like pambazos, tortas filled with mashed potatoes and chorizo bathed in guajillo sauce, and carnitas gorditas, fried masa pouches stuffed with meat. They opened Mezcalero a year later, adding more seafood delights like oysters and ceviche, and portraying a wider realm of regional Mexican cuisine.

Top: Charbroiled oysters. Photo courtesy of Scott Suchman. *Center:* Siblings and chefs Alfredo and Jessica Solis. Photo courtesy of Anafre. *Bottom:* Anafre's seafood sampler. Photo courtesy of Scott Suchman.

As the duo has expanded their empire, they've never stopped drawing upon their roots and upbringing. Seafood-focused Mariscos 1133 reflects Alfredo's treasured childhood memories of years spent on the Mexican coast with his family. Anafre, meaning "portable oven" in Spanish, is an ode to the stove their mother cooked on while Alfredo and Jessica grew up in the countryside. An emphasis is placed on the coastal dishes of Baja California and the Yucatán Peninsula.

The siblings' affinity for spicy food is evident in how they cook and eat. Alfredo's favorite ingredients to work with are spicy peppers, and it's rare to spot either Solis sibling without a bottle of spicy salsa in hand—they carry it with them wherever they go. When it comes to spicing up DC's culinary landscape, the brother-and-sister team seem to have arrived right on time.

El Sol Restaurante & Tequileria
1227 11th St. NW, 202-815-4789
262 Cedar Ln., Ste. C, Vienna, VA
703-712-7701
elsol-dc.com

Mariscos 1133
1133 11th St. NW, 202-836-4107
mariscos1133.com

Mezcalero
3714 14th St. NW, 202-803-2114
8368 Richmond Hwy., Alexandria, VA
571-347-7995
mezcalero-va.com

Anafre
3704 14th St. NW, 202-758-2127
anafredc.com

OPEN CRUMB

Advanced West African home cooking where less is deliciously more

Peter Opare grew up in his family's restaurants watching his parents, who were always at the forefront of the industry. While many were drinking household staples like Folgers in the '90s, Peter's parents were the region's first to offer specialty coffee. When a group visited their coffee shop after a Peace Corps assignment in Ghana, Peter's mother, Abigail, invited them to return the following week for a traditional Ghanaian meal. She wasn't doing it for money; she genuinely wanted to share the food of their homeland. As they regaled in Abigail's feast, so did many others. A newfangled restaurant concept had been birthed while unknowingly sealing her son's destiny.

Peter began helping in the kitchen when he was 10 years old. He gradually learned how to cook, eventually offering his own suggestions for improvements. Whenever Peter would ask to dine out, his mother notoriously reminded him that "they had food at home," so he learned how to prepare the foods that he craved. After noting how much he loved the clam chowder during a trip to Boston, his mother purchased the ingredients that he needed so that he could replicate the New England specialty. Yes, Peter learned the art of cooking from his mother, but he also learned the invaluable impact of being loved, nurtured, and supported.

Peter dove into the world of professional cooking in Anacostia. While the eponymous neighborhood is one of the District's oldest, it's also somewhat of a food desert. Peter set out to change that, working tirelessly to bring high-quality ingredients and scratch cooking to the community. He makes everything in-house, including the bread, which he vehemently believes is the most important element of any

Top left: Fried chicken sandwich with special sauce. *Above left:* Roasted brussels sprouts with seasoning and finished with lemon and vinegar. *Top center:* Red Red, a combination of fried plantains and bean stew. *Above center:* Open Crumb's crave-worthy crab cake sandwich. Photos courtesy of Curt Camron. *Right:* Open Crumb chef and owner Peter Opare. Photo courtesy of William Opare.

sandwich. He blends most of his own spices too, noting paprika and turmeric among his favorites. Every aspect of Peter's cooking is intentional. He doesn't add extra ingredients or sauces for the sake of adding them. At Open Crumb, it's clear that less is deliciously more.

Growing up, Peter sometimes pushed back on his cultural roots, but today, the gifted chef audaciously leans in. His cooking serves as a tool he uses to honor his West African roots, meticulously balancing what the community may be accustomed to with the flavors and foods of his ancestors. Don't miss his exceptional jollof rice, shrimp and grits, or fried or grilled chicken marinated in Greek yogurt, a nod to the Lebanese community Abigail where grew up back in Ghana.

1243 Good Hope Rd. SE, 202-610-9979
opencrumbdc.com

Open Crumb offers takeout and delivery services; no sit-down dining is available. Check out their catering menu to order larger platters. Savory stews like spinach, chicken, goat, fish, and oxtail, along with other soul-soothing stars like mac-and-cheese bites and kelewele, dried fried plantains seasoned with spices, lend to a mouthwatering menu.

SHABABI PALESTINIAN ROTISSERIE CHICKEN

A reclamation of heritage, food, and home

Sometimes you need to leave somewhere so that you can eventually return. Chef Marcelle G. Afram did just that when they left their home in hopes of becoming more autonomous and finding their way in the world. Ultimately, Marcelle found their way back home, returning to their roots and reclaiming their heritage along the way.

Meaning "my people" in Arabic, Shababi Palestinian Rotisserie Chicken honors the Palestinian family, culture, and food that have impacted Marcelle's life. Marcelle's parents emigrated from Lebanon and Syria to the US in the 1970s, settling in Silver Spring, Maryland. Marcelle entered the restaurant industry at age 10, working at the mom-and-pop restaurants that their parents owned across the region. They continued to gravitate toward cooking into their teens, poring over cookbooks and working in more formal establishments. Later, Marcelle traveled the world, spending time on fishing boats in Puerto Rico, cooking in Michelin-starred restaurants in Spain, and cooking over wood fires in a Wisconsin beef cooperative.

Upon returning to DC, Marcelle embarked upon a distinguished career, including stints as the executive chef of Michelin-starred Maydān and sister restaurant Compass Rose. After some time, the notoriety and accolades earned through these high-profile roles were no longer a priority. Marcelle wanted to pursue a higher purpose: cooking the food of their people while making their ancestors proud. Marcelle recalls being discriminated against because of their heritage and their parents understating Arabic flavors in their cuisine in hopes of assimilating. Marcelle is acutely aware of the privileges and responsibilities that come

Left: Shababi's bounty of flavors and delights. *Right:* Founder and chef Marcelle Afram and their wife, Joyce Miller. Photos courtesy of Farrah Skeiky.

with being a firstgeneration American. As the grandchild of Palestinian refugees expelled from their homes in 1948, Shababi was conceived as a reclamation of their Palestinian culture and a remembrance of their family's participation in the diaspora.

Shababi opened as a pop-up in 2023 at a friend's deli in Alexandria, Virginia. The family business includes wife Joyce at the helm of operations and their son as sous-chef. Shababi's main star is their rotisserie chicken inspired by musakhan, Palestine's national dish. The chicken is brined for an entire day and then coated with a mixture of spices including sumac, cumin, and cardamom. The slow-cooked chicken is served with Shabibi taboon, a Palestinian flatbread that's traditionally baked in a clay oven.

As Marcelle fondly reflects upon the stories that their grandfather would tell of eating musakhan along the West Bank, they can't help but feel proud of their food hitting similar notes suggestive of home.

info@shababichicken.com, 571-303-9651
shababichicken.com

In addition to their pop-ups, Shababi is available for catering, private dinners, luncheons, neighborhood drops, and other dining events. Request forms are available on their website.

MAGPIE AND THE TIGER

Follow the unconventional and playful path for extraordinary Korean cuisine

Husband-and-wife team Caleb Jang and Roren Choi shared strong connections long before meeting each other at Momofuku DC years ago. Both are steadfast in honoring their Korean and American heritages, and during their younger years both found themselves turning to the Food Network's *Good Eats* with Alton Brown to learn about the art and science of cooking.

While Caleb and Roren initially pursued studies and careers outside of cooking, both were ultimately drawn to the culinary world. Food has always been a way to delve deeper into their Korean roots, a medium for learning more about their culture and also about themselves. From taking on a side job as a barista to learn more about coffee to stodging at restaurants to sharpen her knife skills, Roren sought out any opportunity that she could to further expand upon her craft. Caleb cooked at an onslaught of eateries to hone his culinary skills, including an early stint at Chipotle before venturing into more esteemed establishments like Himitsu and Moon Rabbit. Eventually, the couple pulled from their diverse backgrounds to open their own restaurant, Magpie and the Tiger.

Their brick-and-mortar was short-lived, closing only seven months after opening. Their devotion and enthusiasm, however, remained, steering them onto an unconventional path that affords them the opportunity to be more playful within their métier. After hosting a private dinner for their loyal supporters, they realized how much they loved connecting with a more intimate group while being able to curate customized dining experiences. Their tailored dinners provide an opportunity to integrate the Korean food they

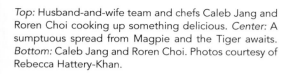

love to cook and eat in an intentional and individualized way. Roren and Caleb explain that they are no longer confined to the conventions and limitations often associated with running a restaurant. Their distinctive dining concept lends to an experience that feels special and extremely personal. As Caleb notes, "It's like going to a restaurant and choosing exactly what you want to eat." The polished pair have intentionally designed it that way, as they never repeat a menu and meticulously design every aspect based on the party's preferences.

In addition to private dinners, Roren and Caleb love to collaborate with fellow DC chefs and catering friends for pop-up dinners, long-term residencies, and other partnerships that push the envelope and challenge the status quo. The driven duo has also taken their talents abroad, including recent pop-up events in Seoul.

info@magpieandthetiger, magpieandthetiger.com

Email Magpie and the Tiger to book your next at-home dining experience. Multicourse Korean barbecue feasts require a minimum of six guests and an outdoor area that can accommodate a grill and guests.

BUFFALO & BERGEN | DESIGNATED DRINKER SHOW

Shaking things up

Buffalo & Bergen and Last Call owner Gina Chersevani may be known for her larger-than-life personality, but there's an even bigger heart underneath all her moxie. Of course, she cares about the thousands of things that go into running a successful establishment. But what Gina *really* cares about is what's being cultivated within her four walls: a welcoming space where people can create memories and celebrate milestones, and where nostalgia and nourishment go hand in hand. As she emotionally shares, when someone chooses you, it's your responsibility to honor that choice and provide them with something real.

Buffalo & Bergen is a love letter to Gina's mom and close-knit family. Her mother grew up in Brooklyn spending hours hopping from one soda shop to the next in search of the perfect egg cream. None, however, seemed to rival the one at Norma's, the one her mother cherished above all. Years later, Gina realized that it wasn't so much the egg creams that her mother loved, but rather the memories created there. She named Buffalo & Bergen after the corner streets her mother grew up on and put her own spin on the traditional soda shop. Classics like homemade knishes, egg creams, and ice cream floats rule the roost, while New York bagel sandwiches and brunchy cocktails add a delightfully modern twist. Its most ambitious item is its genius Lox'd and Loaded, a Bloody Mary jewel of a drink crowned with their favorite lox bagel.

While Gina is widely regarded as one of the area's leading mixologists, she's proven that she's also an incredibly talented chef, winning a Food Network show, *Guy's Grocery Games*, in November 2022.

Left: Lox'd and Loaded. Photo courtesy of Buffalo & Bergen. *Right:* Hosts Gina Chersevani (left) and Louise Salas (right). Photo courtesy of the *Designated Drinker Show.*

Two bold libation-loving women meet in a bar and birth a beautiful partnership. It all started in 2009 when Louise Salas, Missing Link cofounder and podcast host extraordinaire, met Gina at PS 7's. Gina was leading a cocktail class and invited patron and then-stranger Louise to join. Louise happily obliged and the two have been shaking things up ever since. Well over a decade later, the duo has recently entered their sixth season of cohosting the *Designated Drinker Show,* a spirited podcast that raises the bar on craft cocktails and invites its listeners to come under the influence. Episodes dive into the stories and passions of their Designated Drinkers while Gina whisks up bespoke cocktails that embody each guest. The result is a flavorful concoction of wit, humor, and zeal.

Buffalo & Bergen
1309 5th St. NE, 202-543-2549
240 Massachusetts Ave. NE, 202-525-3355
3501 Connecticut Ave. NW
buffalobergendc.com

Last Call
1301-A 4th St. NE
202-543-2051
lastcallbardc.com

Suburbia
1309 5th St. NE
suburbiabar.com

Designated Drinker Show
designateddrinker.show

HALF-SMOKES

The capital city's symbolic sausage

Philadelphia has its cheesesteak, Chicago has its deep-dish pizza, and Washington, DC, has its half-smoke, a spicy and smoky sausage typically made from a combination of ground pork and beef stuffed into a natural casing. While there are many takes on the iconic staple, a half-smoke is typically smoked before it's grilled, served in a soft white bun, and topped with flavorful fixings like cheese, onions, and chili. One scrumptious bite is enough to know this symbolic sausage goes beyond your run-of-the-mill hot dog.

One would be remiss not to mention legendary Ben's Chili Bowl when listing DC's best half-smokes. The renowned DC institution catapulted the half-smoke into notoriety. Hungry enthusiasts continue to flock to this venerable standby for over 60 years.

Hip and Insta-worthy HalfSmoke adds a bit of panache to the DC classic with its younger following, boozy cocktails, and funky atmosphere. Their signature sausage comes with bacon, mustard slaw, chili, beer cheese, and onion crisps. Other halfsmoke offerings include their Fight for Old DC, a combination of Italian sausage and fire-braised pork smothered in bacon, marinara, peppers, and caramelized onions; and Chappelle's Show, a spicy chicken andouille sausage topped with fig jam, arugula, and honey. The U Street Hipster also offers a plant-based sausage with chimichurri and spiced avocado spread.

Barbecue joint DCity Smokehouse's space may be small, but they deliver big when it comes to flavor and spice. Their namesake half-smoke is blanketed in brisket chili, cheddar-jack cheese, red onions, and mustard. Because sometimes you crave even more soul-satisfying grub, the smokehouse's signature mac and cheese is a fan favorite.

Left: Half-smokes on the grill. Photo courtesy of Ben's Chili Bowl. *Right:* Half-smoke with fries at Ben's Chili Bowl. Photo courtesy of Joshua Cogan.

Georgetown butcher shop Stachowski's Market serves up enormous deli sandwiches that are essentially two meals in one. The compact and consistently busy neighborhood spot is what deli dreams are made of: freshly made, nostalgic sandwiches without the fuss (have I mentioned that they're gigantic?). Their half-smokes are a bit more manageable in size, topped with thinly sliced onions, mustard, and pickle.

Meats and Foods got its start in an apartment kitchen before taking its house-made half-smokes, bacon, and handmade tortillas to its current brick-and-mortar location. The tiny operation is run by two people, so don't be surprised if you're waiting in line for a bit (plus the food here is ridiculously good, so there's that, too!). Their half-smoke is a spicy combination of pork and beef sausage. Veggie and vegan sausages are equally spectacular.

HalfSmoke
Multiple locations
651 Florida Ave. NW, 202-986-2079
halfsmoke.com

You can also find HalfSmoke sausage at Ben's Chili Bowl, DCity Smokehouse, Stachowski's Market, and Meats and Foods.

41

BALANGAY

Soul-satisfying cooking from the Philippines

Named for the ancient wooden boats of the Philippines, Balangay is the prized creation of Filipino Erwin "Wing" Villarias and a loving tribute to the rich history and culture of his revered homeland. When asked to describe why he became a chef, the Palawan Island–born chef pauses, searching for words capable of describing the immense joy it brings to his life. Finally, he settles on this: "Cooking is an unbelievable feeling that satisfies my soul." One bite of Chef Wing's ingenious cooking and your soul will be satisfied, too.

Chef Wing is one of seven children, and his mother taught him how to cook at a young age and bestowed upon him the responsibility of cooking for his siblings. His mom instilled the value of being imaginative by sharing many tricks and techniques. One creation that Chef Wing loved combined household ingredients like boxes of ramen with fresh vegetables from their garden. Another favorite that he learned from his mother is dinuguan, a hearty Filipino stew of pork meat and innards simmered in blood, vinegar, and spices. Wing went on to study restaurant management and worked as a sous-chef before immigrating to the US in 2013.

While Wing worked various jobs, including dish washing at the Natural History Museum, cooking was always his true love. He began cooking dishes infused with island flavors from home for free, handing out samples to local elementary schools and other entities, in hopes of growing his cooking skills while sharing his culture's cuisine. The 2022 Embassy Chef Challenge brought the budding chef to prominence when he won the "People's Choice Award" for his best-selling chicken inasal, a succulent grilled chicken that's marinated for 24 hours in lemongrass, coconut milk, ginger, and turmeric.

Left: Chicken inasal. *Center:* Kinilaw. *Right:* Chef Wing won the Embassy Chef Challenge of 2022 at the Smithsonian. Photos courtesy of Balangay.

In 2017, Chef Wing debuted his first pop-up at shuttered Sally's Middle Name followed by subsequent pop-ups at Coconut Club and Big Bear Cafe. His longest residency has been at H Street's Bullfrog Bagels, where the overwhelmingly positive response he received turned a three-month tenure into a 17-month run.

Nosh on appetizers like turkey lumpia, fried spring rolls filled with ground turkey, vegetables, and atchara (pickled papaya); and ensaladang talong, Chef's take on the Filipino classic grilled and smoked eggplant salad composed of pea shoots, tomatoes, blackened garlic sauce, jicama, crispy yuca, fried shitake, and pickled fresno. Feast on main courses like his famous chicken inasal and roasted duck. Whatever you choose to order, your taste buds will thank you.

3607 Georgia Ave. NW
balangaydc.com

Chef Wing's Filipino-focused fare is available for pickup and delivery as well as for catering intimate and larger-scale events. Don't sleep on Balangay's breakfast and lunch offerings like tosilog–pork tocino (belly), fried egg, sinangag (garlic fried rice), and smoked cherry tomatoes–and tortang talong, an eggplant omelet served with rice and banana ketchup.

SIP AND SAIL DC

A sip of luxury awaits aboard *Cru Classé*

Oenophiles, foodies, and Francophiles, rejoice! Your dream French-inspired waterside escape awaits aboard the *Cru Classé*, a 47-foot sailing yacht located at the Wharf. Michelin Star chef and veteran sommelier Troy Knapp has tapped into his 35 years of restaurant experience and longtime love of the water to curate a distinct food-and-wine experience along the Potomac River. Knapp's calling to the water goes beyond the local waterways. He competed professionally in Jet Ski freestyle back in the 1990s, ranking fourth in the world before going on to perform in water ski shows as a stunt performer. It's only fitting that he would find his way back to the water to share his ardor and prowess with others.

From the initial meet-and-greet to the intimate one-table restaurant setting on board, guests will be treated to a luxurious affair from start to finish. Every element contributes to a purposeful outing and an experiential escape from the typical dining venture. The immaculate sailing vessel exudes tranquility; every detail evokes the sea and its marine life. Chef Knapp's goal is to provide a level of hospitality and indulgence that diners would expect at their favorite restaurant while being enveloped by calming water and natural beauty.

All experiences are private; guests can choose from two nautical experiences: the Cru Classé Cruise Experience or the Champagne and Oyster Cruise. Cru Classé is a 2.5-hour cruising experience where guests will enjoy a four-course cuisine package. Aboard the 1.5-hour Champagne and Oyster Cruise, guests will enjoy local oysters and prestige champagne. The ingredients are inspired by locality and seasonality and reflect Knapp's commitment to sustainability. Chef Knapp taps into his relationships with local creameries,

Top and center: Cuisine aboard—the FARM and SEA menus are inspired by partnerships with the local artisans and waterman. *Bottom:* On cruise control, sailing DC's local waterways. Photos courtesy of Damon Bowe.

seafood purveyors, and oyster farmers and incorporates those collaborations into his dishes. Knapp's love affair with French culture is unmistakable. His travels through France's wine country and interactions with sommeliers inform each meticulously designed detail. The prestige selection of wines and champagnes from the winehouses of Provence and Bordeaux, along with the French-themed playlists, is designed to evoke the smells, tastes, and sounds of the French countryside and Riviera.

Experiences can be tailored to accommodate a wide range of diners, including gluten-free and vegan. Pricing is itemized and reservations are available for groups up to six. The *Cru Classé* is also available for special occasions, including elopements and engagements, and a photographer can be hired upon request.

650 Wharf St. SW, 202-361-3844
sipandsail.biz

Wine is sold separately via Sip and Sail DC's online menu. Chef Knapp and his crew work with guests to select wine pairings as well as any other needs and requests. Visit their website for bookings and inquiries.

CANE | ST. JAMES

Tastes of Trinidad

Growing up in Trinidad, cooking and entertaining were an integral part of Jeanine Prime's childhood and the centerpiece of every gathering. At 17, Jeanine immigrated to the United States, eventually making her way to DC and joining forces with her brother Peter. Jeanine's strong business acumen combined with Peter's extensive culinary experience proved to be a recipe for success. While scouting out restaurant locations, they were drawn to the revitalization of H Street and the neighborhood's diversity. As fate would have it, they met a couple who were looking to sell their H Street establishment. The siblings seized the opportunity and in April 2019, Cane was born.

The 33-seat restaurant opened to widespread acclaim. Its intimate space and convivial vibe were inspired by the rum shops found throughout Trinidad. As Jeanine shares, the perception of Caribbean cuisine can sometimes be limited; people often think of Jamaican food as being representative of the entire region. On the contrary, Trinidadian fare is diverse, drawing upon influences of East Indian, West African, French, Portuguese, and Spanish flavors. The duo also wanted to expose diners to the tradition of liming, the practice of relaxing with family and friends while enjoying food and drinks. Cane's menu reflects the island's street food as well as many of their family's favorite dishes, including oxtail, pepper pot, curried beef, and jerk chicken. Their popular paratha tiffin boxes, brimming with

> Both Cane and St. James offer expansive catering menus, including a variety of appetizers ordered by the dozen, omnivore and herbivore party packs, proteins, sides, and sauces.

Top left: Jerk wings at Cane. Photo courtesy of Jason Shelton. *Above left:* Fried snapper at St. James. Photo courtesy of Reema Desai. *Top right:* Pepper shrimp at St. James. *Above right:* Paratha roti platter at St. James. Photos courtesy of Melena S. DeFlorimonte.

Indian bread served with an assortment of curries and chutneys, are a nod to old-school Trinidadian lunch boxes, what elders would pack for their children for lunch.

In May 2022, Jeanine opened Cane's highly anticipated sister restaurant, St. James, named after the district of Port of Spain known for its lively nightlife scene. The 67-seat modern Caribbean eatery evokes the brightness and airiness of the Caribbean with rich hues of green and a vibrant palm-leaf mural that spans the length of the wall and extends up to the mezzanine. Its menu highlights both small and shared plates, allowing guests to sample a variety of Trinidadian staples. Dishes are inspired by the distinct ethnic groups that have made the island their home, resulting in a robust menu. Highlights include the callaloo soup, aloo and chana pies, crab and dumplings, pork pow, and their shareable paratha roti platter.

Cane and St. James enthusiastically flaunt the multicultural nature of Trinidad's food, one mouthwatering bite at a time.

Cane
403 H St. NE, 202-675-2011
cane-dc.com

St. James
2017 14th St. NW, 202-627-2981
stjames-dc.com

TEAISM

Steeped in love and accessibility

When trailblazers Michelle Brown and Linda Neumann founded Teaism in 1996, they were among the first to introduce DC not just to fast-casual dining, but also to the notion that tea could extend beyond the commonplace versions found in most grocery stores. They wanted to debunk the misconception that tea was simply powder stuffed into a bag with a string attached or that it was only served in dainty teacups. Together they harnessed their reverence and expertise of exotic loose tea to create an Asian-inspired teahouse where tea is accessible to all.

Hailing from powerhouses like Restaurant Nora and Clydes, Michelle and Linda have a breadth of food and beverage experience that spans decades. Michelle had become increasingly disheartened by a DC restaurant scene that was often characterized by stiff linens and fancy suits. As she pondered her future, she found herself gravitating toward earthier iterations of traditional dining, longing for a space that was free from pretentiousness and exclusivity. Michelle and Linda partnered to create a gathering space grounded in a community where tea could be celebrated and savored. Teaism launched in Dupont Circle and was followed by subsequent locations across the city. While they've evolved throughout the years, their guiding principles remain the same: loose-leaf tea must be accessible to everyone, and its integrity and authenticity must be preserved.

Lela Singh grew up watching her mother Michelle and Linda share their erudition of tea. She was given responsibilities like wiping off tables while gradually learning the business. Today, Lela plays an integral role in operations and helps carry the torch in presenting tea in an Asian context, staying authentic where it matters but not so obsessively that it feels forced.

Left: Loose-leaf chai. *Center:* A lovely lunch served with tea. *Right:* Jasmine crème brûlée. Photos courtesy of Teaism.

Teaism offers over 50 types of loose-leaf tea. Their traditional organic Indian masala chai blend is undoubtedly their most popular. They work with blenders in perfecting the exact ratio of black tea and a combination of warming spices. Their impressive tea list is divided into five categories: black, oolong, white, green, and tisane. Tried-and-true varieties like Moroccan mint are available, as are lesser-known infusions like Guranse, with a similar flavor profile to Darjeeling teas, and Joongjak, a unique Korean green tea. Teaism intentionally carries loose tea without packaging, allowing consumers to have control over how much they're purchasing and brewing.

Teaism's food menu is designed to highlight Asian cuisine that pairs with their distinct teas. Healthy dishes like curries, bento boxes, and Japanese dishes are emphasized.

Multiple locations
Penn Quarter (restaurant and tea shop):
400 8th St. NW, 202-638-7740
teaism.com

SEYLOU BAKERY & MILL

Regenerating the agricultural system one grain at a time

Seylou Bakery & Mill's philosophy is as simple as it is admirable: follow a holistic process that focuses on a regenerative agricultural system that rebuilds soil and supports a flourishing ecosystem. While that may seem like a tall order for a bakery, for husband-and-wife team Jonathan Bethony and Jessica Azeez, it's a way of life and how they've committed to upholding time-honored traditions and techniques. As Jonathan passionately explains, exclusively using whole grains and locally sourced ingredients helps nurture a thriving and integrated ecological system.

Seylou is the area's first and only bakery that operates an in-house mill. Its fresh milling aspect empowers every link of the ecosystem chain while allowing the bakery to use the whole farm so that little to nothing is wasted. One hundred percent of Seylou's whole-wheat flour is milled on-site, and nearly all breads undergo a slow fermentation process. The richly dark-colored loaves emerging from Seylou's Spanish wood-fired oven are imperfectly perfect, and some of the most exceptional breads in the region.

Seylou follows a "living off the land" approach, implementing practices that maximize available crops while applying creative techniques that yield high-quality foods. Seylou has mastered the act of baking nutrient-dense and mouthwatering breads and pastries while reducing its carbon footprint. As Jonathan notes, a healthy land lends to a healthy body; everything is connected and when one aspect prospers, others do, too. Sourcing through local farms also means sourcing through families, as opposed to mass distributors. Jonathan takes great pride in working directly with farms and the hard-working families behind them.

Left: Seylou's whole wheat baked with love and purpose. *Center:* Glorious grains. *Right:* Baguette in a bag. Photos courtesy of Seylou.

The whole-farm model, including grains, eggs, dairy, and oils, is reflected in every aspect of Seylou's menu. Try a loaf of their einkorn bread, an ancient-grain bread with a thin crust and a soft-and-fluffy interior. Einkorn has been cultivated by farmers for over 10,000 years and is touted for its numerous health benefits, including being an excellent source of fiber and protein while being easier to digest. Seylou's gluten-free Bird Bread is a customer favorite, packed with oats, millet, sunflower seeds, flaxseed, sorghum syrup, and olive oil. Other outstanding loaves worthy of a serrated knife include their rye and rustica baguette.

Did someone say pastries? Seylou serves a wealth of sweet riches, including croissants, cookies, scones, and muffins. Just like their superb breads, pastries are baked with 100 percent whole grain, natural ingredients, and lots of love.

926 N St. NW, 202-842-1122
seylou.com

Visit Seylou on Wednesdays from 5 to 7:30 p.m. for pizza night. All pizzas feature a whole-grain sourdough crust with locally sourced grains and toppings. Can't make it to the bakery? Seylou delivers breads, pastries, flours, coffees and teas, and other merchandise within a five-mile radius of their bakery.

LAPIS

Afghan fare rooted in family

In 1987 Shamim Popal and her family fled their home in Afghanistan, leaving behind loved ones in hopes of building a new future for themselves and their three children. Like countless refugees around the world, they found themselves in a new country filled with uncertainty. Determined to ensure that their children held on to their heritage, Shamim enlisted help from her mom and uncle across the globe and began learning how to cook Afghan food. Feeding her family food made from healthy and fresh ingredients was imperative to Shamim. She was determined to cook meals from scratch, rejecting processed foods and fast-food establishments. After hours of cooking lessons, Shamim emerged as her household's primary chef.

A testament to Shamim's revered home-cooked meals, her children suggested that she expand upon her cooking skills and open a restaurant. She and her husband drew on their extensive travels to Europe and love of French cuisine and opened two French-inspired eateries: Café Bonaparte in Georgetown followed by Café Napoléon in Adams Morgan. While their French-influenced establishments were initially niche, eventually the city became saturated with French restaurants, ultimately causing them to change course and return to their Afghan roots.

Shamim recalls sitting with her family in their Adams Morgan establishment being asked to be the chef of their new venture. Feeling the weight of the responsibility that being a chef carried, she initially said no. After a sleepless night and concluding that this undertaking could result in something that she could leave behind to her children, the next day Shamim decided to take the leap and become Lapis's executive chef. Within hours, the restaurant walls were torn down

Top: Lapis's bright and airy dining room and bar. *Center:* Lapis chef and owner Shamim Popal. *Bottom:* Buranee Bademjan. Photos courtesy of Lapis.

and the transformation to an authentic Afghan restaurant was underway. While the restaurant concept drastically changed, the devoted staff stayed the same. Shamim and her family taught their team Afghan names, ingredients, and dishes. She feverishly handwrote the recipes she cooked for her family in her recipe book, a practice she continues to follow today. She continues to study and employ the flavors of home, relying heavily on spices like turmeric, ginger, and sumac. Mirroring Shamim's home kitchen, you won't find any processed or canned ingredients at Lapis. Over 35 years after leaving Afghanistan, Shamim and her family are as dedicated as ever to cooking exclusively with fresh and halal ingredients and sharing their culture and cuisine with the surrounding community.

1847 Columbia Rd. NW, 202-299-9630
lapisdc.com

Lapis is open for lunch, dinner, and weekend brunch. They also provide catering for both small and large events. Visit their website to learn more.

FISHSCALE

Go wild and cast your net on some of the District's most flavorsome fish

Brandon Williams's introduction to cooking grew out of a love for food and a two-working-parent household. Brandon understood the demands of his parents' careers, so he began dabbling in the kitchen and taught himself how to cook. After he went on a youth-group fishing trip to the Chesapeake Bay, his aunt cooked the fish he caught, and it was love at first bite. While Brandon was young, he knew this fish was different. This indelible moment taught the budding chef that local and fresh is unequivocally *better*.

Brandon's zeal for healthy and sustainably sourced food was inspired by the book *Natural Cures*. He dove into an arduous study of how the food he and his family enjoyed was sourced, grown, and raised. His mother was a pescatarian, and he wanted to ensure that she avoided farm-raised fish. Brandon frequented international markets to discover more exotic fish and sought out sustainable wild-caught types of seafood that had been harvested directly from the oceans, rivers, or lakes, and had never lived in captivity.

One July Fourth celebration, Brandon wanted to cook a special fish burger for his mother's birthday. His wild-caught fish burgers were devoured by all, including his carnivore guests. His parents recognized Brandon's immense cooking talent and encouraged him to enroll at

No need to fish around any further! Dive in and satisfy all of your denizen-of-the-deep dreams by ordering carry-out, pickup, or delivery. The small eatery also has a smattering of tables for dine-in seating.

Left: FishScale owner and chef Brandon Williams. Photo courtesy of FishScale. *Center:* True Blue Maryland Crab Burger with spicy sambal and sunflower yogurt coleslaw. Photo courtesy of Deb Lindsey. *Right:* Jerk salmon cheesesteak. Photo courtesy of Anela Malik.

L'Academie de Cuisine Culinary School. There Brandon honed his craft and learned traditional French techniques as well as the ins and outs of running a business. Brandon went on to launch FishScale at the Farmers' Market by the White House. Within a mere six weeks, the *Washington Post* published a rave review, prompting Brandon to take the plunge and open a brick-and-mortar spot in Shaw.

Entering FishScale, you're greeted by a friendly and knowledgeable team who take pride in their house-made fish burgers devoid of any fillers or breadcrumbs. Each day, Brandon purchases his fresh fish; and a list of the daily catches is prominently displayed. Menu mainstays include blue catfish, True Blue Maryland crab, and rockfish. Other catches might include mahi-mahi, sockeye salmon, and porgy. Sandwich sensations include the True Blue Maryland crab burger, composed of succulent, pan-seared Maryland crab topped with a choice of house-made condiments. The Chesapeake Cheesesteak is an absolute knockout. The stellar sandwich bursts with seasoned, skillet-fired fish smothered in caramelized onions, green peppers, provolone cheese, and a dreamy drizzle of garlic aioli.

637 Florida Ave. NW, 202-780-7886
wearefishscale.com

IMMIGRANT FOOD

"Gastroadvocacy" and the immigrant story

Diners at Immigrant Food, DC's first cause-casual restaurant, can feel good about supporting immigrants while simultaneously enjoying a sensational meal. Immigrant Food is a gastronomic whirlwind celebrating the wealth of culinary riches that immigrants have brought at a more refined level. Guests are treated to a smorgasbord of shareable plates that combine ingredients, spices, and preparations from around the globe. The result is a harmonious blend of diverse cultures, cuisines, and cocktails in a whimsical space.

Michelin Star Chef Enrique Limardo's creation unites food, community, and advocacy. Menus vary based on location, but the overarching concept remains the same: honoring the many distinctive dishes and contributions of immigrants and the lands they come from. A myriad of bites, street food, bowls, sandwiches, and plates represent nearly every corner of the world. Guests craving Asian fare have a bevy of dishes to choose from like tuna tataki, Thai steak, banh mi, samosas, Korean burgers, and octopus takoyaki. Latin American flavors come to life in their Venezuelan tequeños, vegan chaufa, Havana sandwiches, and sweet churros. Diners who gravitate toward Middle Eastern and African flavors can choose from offerings like Persian plants and peas, West African gumbo, and falafel bocadillo. Vegans and vegetarians, rejoice! There is an abundance of plant-centric eats to dig into. Their lists of international wine, beer, and cocktails include caipirinhas, negronis, Singapore Slings, and much more.

Immigrant Food's pledge to elevate immigrants reaches far beyond its food and drinks. The establishment shares its space with immigrants, hires immigrants, and partners with organizations dedicated to helping and engaging immigrants. Each week, Immigrant Food

Top left: The dining room's world map backdrop. *Above left:* A kaleidoscope of global delights. *Right:* Tuna tataki. Photos courtesy of LB.Kennedy for Immigrant Food.

shares five ways to engage with immigrants with their subscribers. The Engagement Menu highlights regional opportunities centered around volunteering, education, advocacy, and making donations. Their monthly editor's note, *The Think Table*, highlights noteworthy immigrants and their countless contributions.

Immigrant Food's seating configuration is designed to imitate how different cultures convene around the table. The prominent world map that serves as the space's backdrop offers a conspicuous reminder that food has the power to bring people together. Regardless of origin or preparation, food regularly serves as an expression of love, connection, and heritage. Immigrant Food reminds us that no matter where you come from, the act of breaking bread is one that we all share, a commonality that holds the power to break barriers and build bonds.

Multiple locations
Main location: The Planet Word Museum: 925 13th St. NW, 202-888-0760
immigrantfood.com

PIE SHOP

Sweet, sweet melody

A pie shop simultaneously serving as a music concert venue may sound a bit unconventional, but for Pie Shop owner Sandra Basanti it's a harmonious blend of sweetness, familiarity, and remembrance. Growing up in northern Virginia, Sandra frequently came into the city to attend concerts at legendary music venues like the 9:30 Club. Music has always played a significant role in Sandra's life. It's helped shape who she is and represents the things she loves and cares most about, including her husband, Stevie (who, you may have guessed, is a musician). This tiny hip gem strums the sweetest of symphonies, orchestrating a delicious dance between two of life's greatest pleasures.

The daughter of Sudanese immigrants, Sandra describes herself as a latch-key kid with parents who were always working. That strong work ethic coursed through her veins, as she built her shop from the ground up, even living above it for years so that she and her husband could always be on-site and avoid paying multiple rents. Concertgoers will be interested in knowing that the upstairs concert stage occupies their former bedroom!

Everyone who works at Pie Shop, including Sandra and Stevie, are self-taught with no professional training. The kitchen has become Stevie's domain, where his Irish background is lovingly baked into many of their sweet and savory pies, including their crowd-pleasing Guinness Steak Pie. The shop and its pleasing pies are intentionally rustic, reflecting tastes of tradition and home. Patrons can dig their forks into a multitude of vintage, time-tested fillings like apple, pecan, sweet potato, and pumpkin. For those looking to experiment with different sweet combinations, choose from scrumptious slices like s'mores pie and Samoa cookie pie, inspired by the excess of Sandra's daughter's Girls Scout Cookie boxes that have piled high around

Top left: Caramel apple crumble pie. *Above left:* Spinach and goat cheese quiche. Photos courtesy of Rachel A Sale. *Top right:* Pie Shop stage bar. Photo courtesy of Aiden Korotkin. *Above right:* Traditional apple slice. Photo courtesy of Rachel A Sale.

the house. Seasonal rounds of bliss like their Key lime pie have garnered a devoted following including loyal customers who have them shipped all the way to Florida! Notice notes of sweetness, tang, and a sliver of irony. Savory stunners include tofu curry, barbecue pulled pork, and the moechella, a pie packed with sweet and smoky mumbo-marinated slow-cooked shredded chicken.

The upstairs concert venue echoes Sandra's earlier concert days, offering all-ages shows five nights a week. She's proud of the space she's created for lesser-known bands to perform and get exposure. This melodious culmination has come full circle for Sandra, just like their delectable circular counterparts below.

1339 H St. NE, 202-398-7437
pieshopdc.com

Pie Shop's upstairs space and outdoor patio are available for private events for up to 100 people. Their food truck can be found at festivals throughout the region or reserved for events like apartment-building gatherings and more. All inquiries should be submitted through their website.

ELCIELO

A dazzling spectacle of Colombian fare

For a theatrical dining experience, head to Elcielo, the fourth culinary offshoot of the Elcielo restaurant chain created and founded by renowned Colombian celebrity chef and entrepreneur Juan Manuel "Juanma" Barrientos. Located in La Cosecha's Latin American Marketplace, Elcielo joins the ranks of its sister restaurants in Medellín, Bogotá, and Miami and pays homage to Barrientos's native home. Cutting-edge and ancestral cooking techniques come together here, inviting guests to come along on a gastronomic journey that spans from Medellín to Washington, DC.

At Elcielo, carefully prepared dishes are performers in a spectacle that commands the audience's attention. The remarkable level of precision and ingenuity is evident in each of the 22 courses featured in the inventive tasting menu. Small bites, palette cleansers, main entrées, an intricate coffee course, and multiple desserts round out the "sensory immersion" experience. Barrientos's love for his homeland is evident in every curated dish. The meal begins with several amuse-bouches and mini-cocktails like the passion-fruit mistela before heading into light but luscious bites like the crab empanada, uni donuts, and corn buñuelos. Signature dishes include the Tree of Life, a crispy yucca bread mounted upon a wire bonsai tree representing the lungs of the world, the Amazon Rainforest; and the buzzworthy

Elcielo's Chef's Choice menu, a shortened menu of 10 courses, is available on Wednesdays and Sundays. Popular signature courses like the Tree of Life and "choco-therapy" are featured. Dietary restrictions and allergies can be accommodated.

Left: Tree of Life. Photo courtesy of Andrea Grieco. *Center:* Chef Juanma. *Top right:* Grab a seat! A meal of a lifetime is about to begin. Photos courtesy of Mario Alzate. *Above right:* Hold out your hands! "choco-therapy" makes everything better. Photo courtesy of Natalia Aguilera.

"choco-therapy," where diners "wash" their hands in liquid chocolate to awaken all five senses. Larger plates like the yuca gnocchi and seafood cazuela round out the lavish menu.

Perhaps the most playful dessert course is "Lick Me!," a sumptuous slather of creamy goodness that is meant to be licked off the plate. Don't be shy—everyone else who ordered the tasting menu is doing the exact same thing. The course is intended to be ridiculously silly while simultaneously tantalizing your taste buds.

In addition to the extravagant Elcielo Experience, two other experiences are offered. The Journey tasting menu is an abridged version, including 13 of the 22 courses, while the Bar Experience offers a four-cocktail tasting menu as a pairing with a variety of snacks and bites or a choice between eight á la carte dishes. All experiences must be booked and paid for in advance.

The modernistic Colombian establishment has certainly earned its fair share of accolades. Elcielo, Washington, DC, won its first Michelin Star in 2021.

1280 4th St. NE, 202-569-9855
elcielowashington.com

REPUBLIC RESTORATIVES

Outspoken. Disruptive. American.

In more recent years, women have been breaking glass ceilings in the food and beverage industries, among many others. One industry that remains overwhelmingly male dominated, however, is the distillery world. So how did two women with limited experience and no generational wealth or family legacy to fall back on not only break but utterly *smash* the good-ol'-boy distillery ceiling? Grit, drive, savvy, and help from thousands of people who believed in them and their vision nearly as much as they believed in themselves.

When it came to opening a distillery, Republic Restoratives cofounders Pia Carusone and Rachel Gardner had had their fair share of being overlooked and dismissed by others. There was the bank that nearly laughed them out of a loan application meeting and the numerous individuals who would address the men in the room as opposed to speaking to them when discussing business matters. The bold and persistent women were undeterred, however, and decided to take matters into their own hands. On a Sunday morning in 2015 they posted a video campaign asking for the support of investors on social media. By Monday morning, the bank that had previously ignored them was now reaching out. They, along with countless others, had seen the enormous outpouring of support all over the news. Pia and Rachel had not only hit their fundraising goal, they had *crushed* it. They raised a staggering $120,000, becoming the largest crowdfunded distillery in US history. The duo had been given the financial and confidence boost they needed to move forward and change DC's distillery landscape forever.

Their built-from-the-ground brand is a celebration of their outspoken and disruptive attitude and their willingness to challenge the status quo. Politically charged spirit names like Madam, a blend

Left: Borough Bourbon. *Center:* Dissent Gin. *Right:* Madam, a blend of whiskies. Photos courtesy of Republic Restoratives.

of seven-year-old bourbon and five-year-old rye, honors America's first female vice president, while Dissent, uniquely crafted gin characterized by atypical ingredients like pepper and allspice, pays tribute to late Supreme Court Justice Ruth Bader Ginsburg. Assembly Gin commemorates the freedom to assemble peacefully, and Civic, the Washington Nationals' official vodka, encourages its drinkers to be unafraid of challenging convention. Republic's Borough Bourbon will make any old-fashioned sing, and their ready-to-drink bottled cocktails (try their Negroni!) are designed to delight even the most discerning palate.

Don't miss Republic Restorative's weekend distillery tours for the chance to taste three of their spirits while learning about the distilling process and touring their Barrel Room.

1369 New York Ave. NW, 202-733-3996
republicrestoratives.com

Republic Restoratives is the only self-distributed distillery in the District. Rather than depending on large trucks, they employ a bike messenger team to quickly deliver their products. Same-day delivery plus an environmentally friendly service equals a winning recipe. In addition to DC, they also ship nationwide.

BEE J'S COOKIES

Batches made in heaven

Bee J's Cookies was birthed out of a love for baking and a deep connection with family. Cofounder and baker Bryant Jones learned the art of baking by watching his grandmother, Sweetie, pick pears off her trees and bake them into scrumptious pies. Bryant soaked up every crumb of his grandmother's passion and knowledge for baking and harnessed it as a love language. Years later, he would bake cookies for his girlfriend Andrea O'Neal, prompting her to suggest that he begin selling his artisan cookies.

Top: Cofounders Bryant Jones and Andrea O'Neal. *Above:* Bee J's cookies. Photos courtesy of SV Images.

The couple launched their cookie business in April 2020, wowing tasters with traditional flavors like chocolate chip, and more unique ones like Florida-inspired sugar cookies with oranges and hints of lemon. Local stores began carrying their cookies, Guinness invited them to customize cookies for them, and they established a pop-up at Union Market. Bryant begins baking at 5:00 a.m. and each day his melt-in-your-mouth treats sell out. As Bee J's Cookies has expanded, they've introduced more personalized flavors that honor the family members who've supported them along the way. Sweetie's Sweet Potato cookie, along with the Brown Sugar cookie, named after Andrea's great-grandmother, Queen, serve as sweet reminders of those who always taste like home.

beejscookies.com

DESTINY'S POPS

Sweet, sweet destiny

At the age of 12, Destiny Pullings, founder of Destiny's Pops, discovered her lifelong passion after attending a six-week summer baking program. She instantly fell in love with baking and launched Destiny's Pops, selling her delectable confections to family and friends. As she grew older and more experienced, her passions evolved, adding cake

Destiny's Pops founder Destiny Graham bakes up a whole lot of sweetness. Photo courtesy of Bonnie Love.

pops, cupcakes, cakes in a jar, cookies, and vegan sweets to her already toothsome creations. Today, you can find her delectable treats at pop-ups like Union Market, as well as order them for birthday parties and other events. Dessert lovers can choose from a bevy of imaginative concoctions like Cookie Me Love and Vegan Lemon Head cake pops and Reese Me and Holy Banana cake jars. Destiny also offers baking classes through her Bake It Up Academy, where she hosts in-person and online classes for students of all ages and levels. Destiny's love for baking was born in a classroom setting, so it's only fitting that she's chosen to pay it forward by offering baking courses in hopes of sparking a passion within others.

Committed to the community and giving back, Destiny and her husband created the Give-a-Cake program where once a year they award a custom cake to someone deserving in the community.

804-888-5257
destinyspops.com

JOSÉ ANDRÉS

Saving the world one philanthropic meal at a time

You don't have to live in Washington, or even the US, to know the immense reach of José Andrés. Chef, restaurateur, philanthropist, and global powerhouse are just a few of the titles that help describe this superhuman and his tremendous impact. While interviewing dozens of chefs, I was touched by how many attributed their growth and success to Andrés. It only makes sense to add mentor and friend to the impressive list of titles Andrés deservedly holds.

Chef Andrés emigrated from Spain at age 21, eventually putting down roots in DC. While volunteering at DC Central Kitchen he expanded upon this work by broadening the role of food and its power to change the world. Following a catastrophic earthquake in Haiti, he founded World Central Kitchen (WCK), a nonprofit organization dedicated to providing meals in the wake of natural disasters. His organization has since grown to epic proportions, providing more than 60 million meals in response to humanitarian, climate, and community crises. From distributing tens of thousands of meals to Texans in response to Hurricane Harvey to providing over 3.6 million meals to hurricane victims in Puerto Rico, Chef Andrés has emerged as one of the greatest humanitarians of our lifetimes. In response to COVID-19, WCK collaborated with thousands of restaurants, farmers, and community leaders to feed families, healthcare workers, and the elderly. The organization has also developed programs to train aspiring chefs and school cooks in skills and safe practices to build careers fighting food insecurity and promoting nutrition.

Jaleo, Andrés's first restaurant in the US, showcases the bold flavors of his native country. Following its success, the revered

Left: Halloumi pide at Zaytinya. *Right:* Octopus Santorini at Zaytinya. Photos courtesy of Rey Lopez.

chef launched a slew of other establishments. Zaytinya represents Andrés's knowledge of Mediterranean cooking acquired during his travels throughout the region; Oyamel celebrates the spirited flavors of Mexican cuisine; and China Chilcano emphasizes the fusion of Peruvian Criollo, Chinese Chifa, and Japanese Nikkei culinary traditions. The Bazaar pays tribute to American fare and history.

Andrés's two-Michelin-starred masterpiece, minibar, revolutionized DC's dining scene, challenging everything we thought we knew about how food can be prepared and experienced. Minibar introduced Washingtonians to molecular gastronomy, where unorthodox cooking techniques grounded in science create innovative dishes that push the envelope of traditional food. The multisensory affair breaks all the rules, presenting ingenious, constantly evolving dishes. Barmini, Andrés's adjacent cocktail lab, flaunts over 100 imaginative libations, as well as curated flights and artful snacks.

For a full list of José Andrés restaurants, visit:
joseandres.com/restaurants

The Bazaar is the brilliant product of a 30-year journey. Since arriving in Washington, DC, in 1993, Chef José Andrés had dreamed of opening a restaurant in the historic Old Post Office Building. His dream finally came true in February 2023.

JOE'S NOODLE HOUSE

Head down the Pike for some of the region's best Chinese food

The DMV boasts a plethora of outstanding Chinese restaurants, and several that are outside the city's borders are well worth the trek. Rockville, Maryland, is often designated as the area's Chinatown, home to some of the region's best Chinese eateries. Rockville's irresistible Chinese cooking scene will have you headed down the Pike and picking up a pair of chopsticks in no time.

Joe's Noodle House has been a regional Szechuan favorite for years. The no-frills establishment's dark and unassuming interior will be forgotten as soon as your food arrives. Portions are huge, so arrive with an empty stomach and plenty of room in your fridge for leftovers. You can't go wrong with any of the spicy noodle soups; the rich-and-fiery beef broth is so incredibly soothing, you'll think you've gone straight to soup heaven. Looking to heat things up even more? The

Top: House pan-fried noodles with tofu and vegetables. *Above:* Soothing beef noodle soup at Joe's Noodle House.

number of chili peppers next to various menu items gives you an idea of the incendiary level, and those denoted with a star indicate "numbing," so proceed with caution (and perhaps a cold glass of milk!). Bountiful dishes like fried noodles brimming with Chinese vegetables, heaping platters of Szechuan green beans, and delicious dumplings help keep tables filled and to-go orders flowing.

1488-C Rockville Pike, Rockville, MD, 301-881-5518
joesnoodlehouse.com

BOB'S SHANGHAI 66

Stuffed and satisfied: dumplings that are simply soup-er

Top: Lamb with cumin and spicy pork wontons. *Above:* Xiao Long Bao (pork soup dumpling.) Photos Courtesy of William La.

Bob's Shanghai 66 has been feeding the DMV for over 20 years. When it opened in 2002, it focused on Taiwanese fare before changing its concept to Shanghai cuisine, which tends to be sweeter and mellower than other regional Chinese cuisines. Bob's loyal following come here for their renowned soup dumplings; try the hugely popular ones filled with regular pork or pork and crab roe. Other standouts include flounder filet cooked in hot chili sauce, Szechuan-style beef stew noodle soup, eggplant with garlic sauce, and stir-fried Shanghai noodle dishes served with choices like chicken or vegetables. You'll find a variety of peppers infused into Bob's dishes, including dry hot peppers, Szechuan peppercorns, and longhorn peppers.

Bob's staff resembles a close-knit family, gathering each day to taste test dishes and enjoy family-style meals together. Shanghai-born Head Chef Ms. Wang leads the team in incorporating regional flavors and cooking techniques into dishes while her brother runs the dumpling station. Bob's diverse clientele has prompted them to "Americanize" several menu items, including Western favorites like General Bob's chicken, a play on General Tso's chicken, and orange chicken.

Be sure to hit the ATM before gorging on their infamous soup-er dumplings; Bob's is a cash-only restaurant.

305 N Washington St., Rockville, MD, 301-251-6652

MUNICIPAL FISH MARKET AT THE WHARF

A tail of history

While venturing to the southwest corner of the city, don't be surprised if you're greeted by throngs of people, purveyors shouting phrases related to prices and cuts, and of course, the pungent smell of seafood permeating the air. If you're looking for the country's oldest fish market, you've come to the right place. Hailed as the nation's oldest continuously operating open-air fish market, the Municipal Fish Market has been a DC fixture since 1805, predating New York City's historic Fulton Fish Market by 17 years. Through the centuries, the market has hosted an ever-changing group of suppliers, including oyster boats, produce vendors, bait and tackle shops, and lumber distributors. In the beginning years, seafood was served directly from fishing boats along the pier. Today the goods are moved into the various stalls along the wharf. Over 200 years after its inception, the fish market continues to be an iconic DC destination and a perennial favorite among hungry visitors craving fresh fish, crabs, and cooked seafood.

While the fish market has been attracting consumers for centuries, its surrounding area has only recently become a bustling destination in itself. The region encompassing the market was mostly demolished during the urban renewal movement of the 1960s. Developers hoped to revive the region with new roads, residential buildings, and outdoor public spaces, displacing low-income residents and destroying many historic buildings, including the fish market. The vendors of the fish market refused to be pushed out, ultimately securing their place when they were able to identify clauses in their original lease

Top: A good day for crabs at the market. Photo courtesy of Skyfox11, Wikimedia Commons. *Center:* The bustling Municipal Fish Market. Photo courtesy of dbking, Wikimedia Commons. *Bottom:* Fresh catches of the day. Photo courtesy of Bien Stephenson, Wikimedia Commons.

guaranteeing them a market space for 99 years. Since then, the market has become a resounding symbol of continuity and tenacity.

In 2017, the first phase of a dramatic transformation to the Southwest Waterfront was unveiled, reestablishing the capital city as a premier waterfront city. Set along a mile stretch of the Potomac River, the shiny new Wharf has reinvented the Southwest region with an abundance of eateries, bars, hotels, and music venues. In October 2022, the second phase of the Wharf development was announced, simultaneously marking the fifth anniversary of its initial grand opening.

The surrounding area continues to evolve, but the fish market has held steadfast to its humble beginnings and colorful history. It has managed to maintain its authenticity and sidestep the perils of becoming a dreaded tourist trap. This seafood stalwart remains a cherished gem beloved by both locals and visitors.

1100 Maine Ave. SW
www.wharfdc.com/fish-market

ARCAY CHOCOLATES

Experience the art of chocolate

Venezuelan master chocolatier Anabella Arcay has been an entrepreneur ever since she was a child, long before she knew the word existed. From painting to designing belt buckles, Anabella has always loved working with her hands, often selling her art to her mother's friends. Decades later, Anabella continues to create masterpieces by hand, one blissful bonbon at a time.

Anabella's passion for making chocolate wasn't inherent as her penchant for craft making was, and when a friend suggested chocolate making to Anabella, she dismissed the idea. But her friend's persistence finally convinced her to enroll in a two-day course. Less than 48 hours later, Anabella recalls feeling "trapped," completely enthralled by the art of making chocolate. A burgeoning chocolatier emerged.

From the beginning, Anabella wanted her chocolates to be unique. She visited artisans throughout Caracas, methodically planning the confections she wanted to produce. She selected molds and products that would distinguish her candies from those of her peers. Orders soon came pouring in; bombones (bonbons), capacillos (chocolate cups), and materos (chocolate flower pots) were among Anabella's specialties. Venezuela's political unrest, however, brought numerous challenges, including a lack of available ingredients. As food became scarcer, Anabella became more resourceful. Years later, she attributes

> Chocolate lovers don't need to choose just one bite-sized ball of bliss! Bonbon boxes ranging from nine to 25 are available to satisfy every craving, from blackberry cardamom and tamarind to matcha and salted caramel.

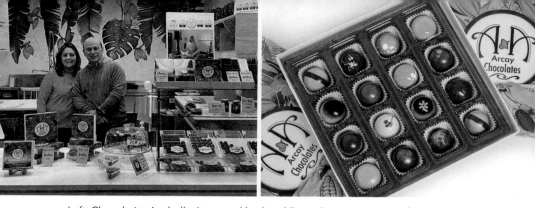

Left: Chocolatier Anabella Arcay and husband Dario Berti, co-owners of Arcay Chocolates. *Right:* Box of assorted bonbons. Photos courtesy of Anabella Berti.

much of her success to her resoluteness and adaptability during those uncertain times.

As Anabella's popularity in Venezuela grew, so did her notoriety around the globe. She was invited to participate in a chocolate fair in Perugia, Italy, and it was here that her career path changed forever. A woman fell head over heels for her passion-fruit bonbons, even going as far as calling her a *strega* (Italian for "witch"), proclaiming that the candy caused her to fall into a trance. She invited Anabella to compete in an international chocolate festival. Two of the five chocolates she entered won: a lemon confection and her trance-inducing passion-fruit flavor. Over five years after competing in her first international competition, Anabella has won a remarkable 42 medals.

Two years after immigrating to DC, Anabella was invited to open a space in La Cosecha. She began experimenting with flavors that appealed to American palates. Bestsellers include rosemary and sea salt, hazelnut, and Oreo bonbons. While her craft has evolved and her clientele has changed, her commitment to steer clear of artificial preservatives and additives has never wavered. By eschewing unnecessary sugars and butter, Anabella upholds the natural color, texture, and taste of her chocolates.

Inside La Cosecha: 1280 4th St. NE
3211 O St. NW, 239-961-8695
arcaychocolates.com

SOUL FOOD CLASSICS

Memorializing Black history and feeding DC's spirit

Satisfying soul food has been feeding the spirit of Washingtonians and commemorating Black history for decades. While its roots have been planted for years, its cuisine continues to flourish and reinvent itself to match the city's constantly evolving food scene. Whether a soul food pioneer like the institutions featured here, or a new(er) kid on the block, all share a common goal: showcasing comforting cuisine with a deep connection to the Black community.

The tips he earned as a Capitol Hill shoeshine man helped Lacey C. Wilson Sr. turn a lifetime dream into a reality. When he opened Florida Avenue Grill in 1944, Wilson wanted to create a homelike space where diners of any race, religion, or culture could enjoy affordable home-style cooking among a trusted community. The Grill became a haven where Blacks could dine comfortably during a time when the country was ravaged by racial conflict. During the 1968 race riots, many businesses were burned to the ground. Lacey refused to succumb to the surrounding destruction, often staying up all night with a shotgun in hand ready to protect his beloved establishment. Holding the title as the world's oldest soul food restaurant, Florida Avenue Grill's legacy lies within its commitment to food and community.

Known for its "Homemade World-Famous Sweet Potato Pie" and fine Southern cooking, Henry's Soul Cafe has been satiating Washingtonians' appetites since 1968. Henry E. Smith originally founded his namesake establishment as a small carryout deli. Dig into a heaping plate of soul food riches here, and make sure to save room for that sweet potato pie.

Trailblazers Al and Adrienne Carter founded Hitching Post Restaurant more than 50 years ago, and the soul food legend has been

Left: All the soul-satisides. *Right:* Comfort food with all the fixings. Photos courtesy of Oohh's & Aahh's.

a stronghold ever since. Barry Dindyal now owns the establishment, maintaining its hospitality and emphasis on Southern food while adding some flavors from his native Guyana. Standouts include the fried whiting, collard greens (which are pleasingly vegetarian), fried chicken, and lemon cake, which tastes like sunshine on a plate.

Since 2003, Oohh's & Aahh's has been a pillar of DC's soul food scene. Local and acclaimed chef Oji Abbott is at the helm of this no-frills eatery, cooking up hearty classics like whiting fish, shrimp and grits, and corn bread. Its signature macaroni and cheese is one of its renowned dishes, striking the perfect balance of indulgence and comfort.

Florida Avenue Grill
1100 Florida Ave. NW, 202-265-1586
floridaavenuegrill.com

Hitching Post Restaurant
200 Upshur St. NW, 202-726-1511
thehpostrestaurant.com

Henry's Soul Cafe
1704 U St. NW, 202-265-3336
5431 Indianhead Hwy., Oxon Hill, MD
301-749-6856
www.henryssoulcafe.com

Oohh's & Aahh's
5933 Georgia Ave. NW, 202-882-2902
1005 U St. NW, 202-667-7142
oohhsnaahhs.com

EASTERN MARKET

Capitol Hill's time-honored tasty town center

Market by name, cultural epicenter at its heart, Eastern Market is the beating pulse of Capitol Hill. This historic public market has been nourishing its devoted community since its completion in 1873. Adolf Cluss, the brilliant architect behind the Smithsonian Arts and Industries Building, was the leading force behind the market's design. The market expanded in the early 20th century when the Center and North Halls were added. The historic market was regarded by many as the "town center" of Capitol Hill.

The market operated continuously until April 30, 2017, when a devastating fire ravaged the building, leaving it severely damaged. City officials and the surrounding enclave immediately came together to rebuild the cherished market, a remarkable testament to its significance and the resilience and commitment of its community. Today, Eastern Market continues to be a thriving cultural hub where neighbors and local vendors share their love for local food, arts, collectibles, flowers, crafts, and antiques.

Steeped in three generations of family tradition, Bowers Fancy Dairy Products has been in operation since it opened in 1964 and has been the community's trusted resource for fresh dairy products ever since. Grandfather Harris Rockford Bowers purchased stand #400 and involved the entire family in its daily operations. Following his passing in 1976, son Ray Bowers took over, working tirelessly each day to honor his father's vision and preserve their family legacy. Today, grandson Mike Bowers has owned and run the cheese shop for more than 50 years after putting his first apron on as a young boy. The shop's future lies with Ryan, the fourth generation of the family to work there, as he follows in his family's footsteps.

Left: Eastern Market and the weekend flea market. *Right:* Eastern Market's iconic Market Lunch.

The Market Lunch has been an Eastern Market standby since 1978. For over four decades the casual corner eatery has been serving up wholesome breakfast platters and comfort-food lunches at their no-frills counter restaurant. Longtime luminaries include their famous blueberry-buckwheat pancakes, crab cakes, and the Brick, a belly-filling breakfast sandwich loaded with egg, potatoes, meat, and cheddar cheese. This is homestyle cooking at its best; locals and out-of-towners have been filling up on their hearty and tasty dishes for years. Two tips: Be sure to hit up the ATM before ordering your French toast as only cash is accepted. And don't let the long line deter you! The line moves quickly, and plates come out fast.

Eastern Market	Bowers Fancy	Market Lunch
225 7th St. SE	Dairy Products	202-547-8444
202-698-5253	202-544-7877	marketlunchdc.com
easternmarket-dc.org	bowerscheese.com	

The more recent addition of the Flea Market at Eastern Market has further elevated the market's appeal and reach, highlighting exhibitors from five continents. The exceedingly popular flea market attracts throngs of visitors every Saturday and Sunday.

MANIFEST BREAD

Handmade with love and grains

High-school sweethearts Tyes and Rick Cook have been in the restaurant industry their entire careers. Their impressive résumés include esteemed establishments like Obelisk and 2 Amys. In 2018 the couple started work on their next culinary venture. Baking bread using a small mill at home began consuming Rick's time. They gave their sourdough loaves to friends for free at first, later charging $5 per loaf. Eventually they took their loaves to Cleveland Park's Weygandt Wines and were an instant hit. They sold out each weekend, and customers began asking them to put aside bread for them. The Cooks continued baking out of their home, responding to the high demand by offering preorders and personally delivering their bread throughout the area.

Tyes and Rick worked with a Realtor, changing course from scouting out large spaces and broadening their search to include smaller spaces outfitted with a front counter. In January 2023, the pair opened their cozy bakery to continued acclaim. Rick traded his small mill for an industrial-sized one, making flour from organic, whole grains sourced from farms in Pennsylvania and on the Eastern Shore. Manifest Bread is one of the few regional bakeries that makes its own flour. Rick explains that conventional all-purpose flour can

> **Did someone say pizza? In conjunction with the Riverdale Park Farmers Market, every Thursday night Manifest Bread does pizza night from 3 to 6:45 p.m. Preorders open at 11 a.m. each Thursday morning for pickup that night. The 16-inch pizza pies include build your own, tomato and anchovy, and pepps on pepps (pepperoni and pepperoncini).**

Top: Bag of grains and goodies. *Center:* Chocolate babka, cookies, bialy, and more perfect pastries to indulge in. *Bottom:* Sourdough, tourte, rye, oh my! Photos courtesy of Laura Whitfield.

typically last for at least a year while their milled flour, which contains no preservatives and additives, has a shelf life of several days. The bread is handmade from start to finish, a process that takes three days. Sourdoughs are baked from organic ingredients and undergo a long fermentation process void of yeast.

Sourdoughs play the leading role at Manifest, with other breads like rye, corny grits, and baguettes playing integral supporting roles. Their corny grits loaf is unique to Manifest and starts off as a sourdough base. Toasted corn polenta is folded in, creating soft pockets of corn, and cracked corn accents the outside. The counter's enclosed case at Manifest is a treasure chest of alluring pastries like their cardamom bun, a mouthwatering brioche-based bun gloriously filled with cardamom and cinnamon, and babka, another brioche beauty embellished with swirls of dark chocolate. Savory treats like bialys are also a delight.

Tyes and Rick's wide range of experiences and travels are woven into many facets of Manifest, including their freshly made to-go sandwiches wrapped in napkins reminiscent of the grab-and-go's they enjoyed during their European sightseeing days.

6208 Rhode Island Ave., Ste. 114, Riverdale Park, MD
manifestbread.com

LEI MUSUBI

Say aloha to Hawaii's favorite snack

Love it or hate it, Spam has been a fixture in millions of home pantries since Hormel Foods Corporation launched it in 1937. The notorious World War II staple has emerged as an American meat icon, selling over a whopping eight billion cans with no signs of slowing down anytime soon. In 2021, Hormel announced record sales of $3.5 billion in a three-month period, with the US and South Korea being its largest markets.

If you're thinking you can't possibly stomach the idea of ordering Spam the next time you're out, consider trying Spam musubi. The all-season, anytime dish consists of a slab of grilled Spam either sandwiched in between or placed on top of a block of rice, bundled together with nori in the custom of Japanese onigiri. The popular Hawaiian snack is loaded with influences from Guam, Japan, Korea, and of course, Hawaii. Portable, affordable, and versatile, Spam musubi has taken the food scene by storm, even making the canned pork concoction a trendy menu item at some of the city's hippest eateries. The Washington, DC, area is home to a wide array of eateries that aren't afraid of experimenting with the 50th state's favorite snack, honoring the multicultural classic with creative and tasty interpretations.

Missing home and her mother's cooking, Vivien Bang created Lei Musubi as a token of love for the food she enjoyed growing up. Bang began to learn her way around the kitchen while serving as her mother's sous-chef during the frequent dinner parties she was prone to host. She attributes her love for cooking as well as her affinity toward experimentation to those early years spent in Hawaii with her mom. Today, Bang has reimagined the rice-and-seaweed bites her mother used to make for dinner and has added her own fresh and inventive spins. Bang's gourmet Hawaiian-style rice balls are as unique and

Left: Unagi drizzle adds the finishing touch at Lei Musubi. *Center:* Handheld goodness at Lei Musubi. *Right:* Tastiness painted with a broad brush at Lei Musubi. Photos courtesy of bakedparktato.

diverse as they are flavorsome. Each rice ball is individually rolled and, as Bang likes to say, "packed with an abundance of flavor and a tsunami of texture." The OG (and its vegan counterpart) combines sticky rice, kimchi, house-made furikake, caramelized Spam, and green tea sea-salted nori, sprinkled with microgreens. Flavors change nearly as much as Bang's food truck locations. Don't be surprised to see nonconventional accompaniments like Flamin' Hot Cheetos and house-made jerk sauce accentuating Bang's latest creations.

Monroe Street Market: 716 Monroe St. NE
leimusubi.com

Visit Lei Musubi's website to see where Bang's food truck is rolling into next. Past and repeated stomping grounds have included Fresh Farm Dupont, Union Market, and at the Monroe Street farmers market in Brookland.

ETHIOPIA COMES TO WASHINGTON

A gastronomic trek through the East African nation

Ethiopian fare has established itself as part of DC's dining landscape. Refugees who fled their war-torn country in the 1970s and '80s settled here and have kept their culinary traditions alive and well. The city became home to so many Ethiopian restaurants near the intersection of Ninth and U Streets NW that the area became known as Little Ethiopia. Ethiopian dishes are typically served communal style on a large platter with options of injera (pancake-like flatbread with a slightly spongy texture) or rice. Scooping up simmering vegetable stews, spicy tibs, and savory legumes with torn-apart pieces of injera makes for a unique dining experience.

Named for the mountains in Ethiopia's West Hararghe zone known for its varied geography, Chercher's menu reflects the region that inspired it. The restaurant is tucked on the second floor of a townhouse a few blocks outside Little Ethiopia. Chercher may be small and minimalist, but their platters deliver a bold and spicy punch. Their popular vegan combo platter (the deluxe special can easily feed three hungry people) is an edible kaleidoscope of regional classics like gomen (collard greens), kik alicha (split peas), and kike we't (spicy lentil sauce). Meat dishes like kitfo, finely chopped sirloin seasoned with butter and chili powder, and geba weta, sautéed short ribs, add to a sensational selection of offerings.

A staple of Little Ethiopia, family-owned Dukem has been serving traditional fare since 1997. A wide selection of both vegetarian and nonvegetarian dishes is offered along with a fully stocked bar. What began as a small carryout business has evolved into a 150-seat

Left: A bountiful spread at Elfegene. *Right:* Elfegene special goden tibs. Photos courtesy of Elfegne.

restaurant with year-round live music and has now expanded to a second location in Baltimore, Maryland.

A meal at Elfegne is suitable for a king, as their name (referring to the regal dining halls where royalty would eat) fittingly suggests. Diners come to this Adams Morgan haunt for their savory tibs—choose from lamb, beef, chicken, and short ribs—as well as their zesty stews simmered with meat, vegetables, lentils, and a medley of exotic spices.

Ethiopic is proud to be the first Ethiopian restaurant in the H Street Corridor. The restaurant's namesake (also known as Ge'ez) is a classical language and ancient script of Ethiopia dating back to fourth century AD, and its decor is influenced by Ge'ez's early scripts. The eatery's vegetarian and beef and chicken samplers are satisfying smorgasbords featuring some of their most popular offerings.

Chercher
3608 14th St. NW, 202-222-0433
4921 Bethesda Ave., Bethesda, MD,
301-652-6500
chercherrestaurant.com

Dukem
1114 U St. NW, 202-667-8735
1100 Maryland Ave., Baltimore, MD,
410-385-0318
dukemrestaurant.com

Elfegne
2420 18th St. NW, 202-667-4700
elfegnedc.com

Ethiopic
401 H St. NE, 202-675-2066
www.ethiopicrestaurant.com

OUR MOM EUGENIA

Greek Goddess of Northern Virginia

Eugenia Markesini Hobson, the restaurant's namesake chef, has been cooking Greek cuisine for over 40 years. A native of Zakynthos, an island off Greece's west coast, she learned how to cook from her mother and also from her grandmother, the woman for whom she was named. Eugenia and her husband, John, met in Athens while John was stationed in Greece with the US Air Force. They later moved and started a family in Manhattan before returning to Athens in the early 1980s. Over the course of several decades, the family eventually made their way back and settled in the States. In December 2016, Eugenia, along with her sons, Alex and Phil, opened their first establishment in Great Falls, Virginia. Its enormous success led to two subsequent locations in Mosaic and Shirlington. So, while we may not be able to jet off to Greece any time we'd like, we *can* make reservations at Our Mom Eugenia, which may just be the next best thing.

Perhaps the best way to jump-start your Grecian food tour is by scooping up one or six (!) of their luscious spreads with a stack of grilled pita triangles. Dazzlers include the taramosalata, a velvety smooth fish roe dip, and tirokafteri, a bold and tangy feta dip enhanced by roasted red peppers and cayenne pepper. A lovely way to continue is to order the vegetarian platter. The sampler includes spanakopita, gigante beans stewed in tomato sauce, patzaria (slowly baked beets served with a pistachio and garlic spread), and imam baildi (roasted baby eggplant with pine nuts, feta, and raisins). Entrées here are plentiful, both in variety and portion size. Thalassina—a hearty seafood stew laden with mussels, shrimp, and calamari served over orzo simmered in white wine, ouzo, and tomato sauce—is as soothing as it is sensational. Fall-off-the-bone oven-braised lamb

Left: A trio of spreads served alongside a classic Greek salad. *Right:* Thalassina, a delicious seafood stew served over orzo.

set upon a bed of orzo along with a mixed grill meat platter lead an all-star lineup of succulent entrées. You will want to leave plenty of room for dessert. Greek classics like baklava and Galaktoboúreko, a milk custard pie with phyllo pastry, are spectacular, and Mom's apple cake a la mode is what Grecian dreams are made of.

The all-Greek wine list features dozens of varieties. If you're thirsty for a refreshing cocktail, the Italicus Spritz is an excellent choice—a blend so pleasantly quenching, you'll feel like a Greek god or goddess.

Multiple locations
Original location: 1025 Seneca Rd., Ste. H, Great Valls, VA, 703-870-7807
ourmomeugenia.com

Catering services are offered for up to 100 guests. Meals and buffet-style offerings can be customized to accommodate both small and larger gatherings, and delivery and food setup is available within a 20-mile radius of your selected restaurant location at no additional cost. Please visit their website for more information.

ANNANDALE'S ASIAN FOOD SCENE

Reflecting the cuisines of a multicultural community

Some of the region's best Asian cuisine can be found outside of the city limits. Annandale, a thriving suburb located 15 miles outside of Washington, is home to a flourishing Asian American community boasting a bountiful supply of Asian-centric eateries. Those on the hunt for affordable authentic Asian fare will have no trouble. Choosing between the profusion of options, on the other hand, may prove much harder.

Diners have been raving about A&J Restaurant's Northern Chinese–style dim sum since 1996. The Annandale and Rockland locations are part of a family-owned chain, with Elaine Tang and her family running the Virginia and Maryland locations. The menu has so many signature dishes that choosing what to order may feel a bit daunting at first. Homemade noodles, steaming soups, delicately wrapped wontons, and pan-fried pot stickers are just the beginning of its vast menu. While you're slurping hearty bowls of comforting soups, make sure to order a plate of A&J's piquant garlicky cucumber salad, the perfect complement to their abundant noodle and rice dishes.

Korean Barbecue goes far beyond the traditional notion of dining. It's more of a multisensory experience, and a delectable one to boot. Enthusiasts are drawn to its long list of virtues: plentiful portions, heaps of tender cuts of meats, and a white-hot tabletop grill sizzling with succulent flavors. Patrons are often treated to a front-row spectacle of their server firing up the tabletop grill to cook cuts of meat, usually marinated in sweet and spicy sauces. Guests can choose from proteins

Left: Searing squid at 9292 Korean BBQ. *Center:* Red bean bread. *Right:* Macarons at Breeze Bakery Cafe. Photos courtesy of Breeze Bakery Cafe.

like beef, chicken, shrimp, and pork belly. A toothsome spread of side dishes including salads, vegetables, and kimchi are typically included in the feast. Annandale has no shortage of trusted Korean barbecue spots. Popular Virginia-based Honey Pig serves standbys like bulgogi as well as rarer cuts like beef tongue. Family-operated Kogiya offers all-you-can-eat, á la carte, and combo menus, as well as meal kits for grilling up Korean barbecue at home. 9292 Korean BBQ is another Annandale go-to, cooking the usual suspects when it comes to meat, along with short rib, beef tartare, and pork neck.

Craving dessert or lighter fare? Head to Breeze Bakery Cafe, a Korean/European-style bakery offering a delightful medley of baked goods, breads, milk snow, and whole cakes. In need of something more substantial and less sweet? Savory items include quesadillas, soups, and salads.

A&J Restaurant
4316 Markham St., Annandale, VA
703-813-8181
1319 Rockville Pike, Ste. C
Rockville, MD, 301-251-7878
aandjrestaurant.com

Honey Pig
Multiple locations, 410-696-2426
honeypigbbq.com

Kogiya
4220 Annandale Rd., Annandale, VA
703-942-6995
kogiya.com

9292 Korean BBQ
7133 Little River Tnpk., unit A
Annandale, VA, 571-378-1440

Breeze Bakery Cafe
4125 Hummer Rd., Annandale, VA, 703-462-9093
breezebakery.com

NADINE BROWN

The DC area's wine icon is at your service

DMV wine legend Nadine Brown's rise to success is remarkable, especially considering how unconventional it's been. Relentless drive, insatiable curiosity, and a wealth of warmth and relatability have helped carve Nadine's path as one of the greatest wine professionals in the region.

Jamaican-born and Puerto Rican–raised, Nadine had never seen, let alone tasted, wine before coming to DC. A bad breakup brought her to DC, where she eventually landed a job as a hostess at Bistro Bis. She immersed herself in the hospitality industry, voraciously reading about wine and later enrolling in a nine-month Wine Captain course. She wrote the owner of Bistro Bis a letter expressing her desire to become a manager, acknowledging that while she didn't know a lot yet, she would do whatever it took to learn. The newly promoted manager soon found herself learning about luxury wines and being invited to taste rare vintages, some dating to 1865. Nadine was captivated by the stories and people behind the wines. She remembers listening to an NPR segment mentioning the year 1865, enthralled by its history and connection to the wine she recently tasted, and acutely aware of the vast disparity between her experiences and those of her ancestors.

In the early 2000s, Nadine discovered that Charlie Palmer was opening a restaurant. She visited the construction site, handed him her résumé, and introduced herself. She came on board as a lead server, also known as a captain, and continued to take advantage of every learning opportunity that she could. She helped the wine team stock shelves and studied wine books during her lunch breaks. As her career evolved and she took over as Charlie Palmer's wine director,

Sommelier Nadine Brown. Photo courtesy of Nadine Brown.

Nadine became a leading expert in American wines. Within minutes of meeting Nadine, it's clear that this is a woman who can talk to anyone. She is charming, personable, and approachable. Moreover, she is genuinely interested in getting to know you. She puts her guests at ease, encouraging them to drink what they like, as opposed to following rigid rules. After an impressive 14-year run at Charlie Palmer's, Nadine ventured out on her own, broadening her reach and sharing her prowess and radiant energy across the region.

Today, Nadine is the Founder of At Your Service, specializing in wine consultations and bespoke events. Among her many roles, she trains hospitality professionals in wine, develops wine lists for restaurants, is a wine judge and journalist, and, well, is a living wine legend.

At Your Service
nbrownwine@gmail.com

AMBAR

Dishing out a banquet of Balkan bites

Every aspect of Ambar celebrates the gastronomical culture of the Balkan Peninsula. From its convivial atmosphere to its vast selection of traditional dishes, Ambar is a perennial favorite among diners. As the first modern, international Balkan restaurant in the region, guests can expect to be treated to a one-of-a-kind, authentic meal.

Ambar's unique Dining without Limits Experience is a culinary adventure like no other. Diners are encouraged to feast upon over 40 dishes with the option to reorder without any limitations. The concept is a contemporary interpretation of a Balkan tradition called "Voz" (meaning "train"). During the 1950s and 1960s, many restaurants offered diners the choice of ordering a Small or Big Train. Ordering the Small Train produced new dishes every ten minutes, while a Big Train delivered new dishes every five minutes. Ambar's limitless menu is inspired by this time-honored tradition, and all but guarantees that no guest will ever leave hungry. The reimagined idea allows individuals to customize their food preferences; patrons can order whatever they want, as often as they want. The only prerequisite required for eating at Ambar is an empty stomach.

Ambar offers unlimited brunch, lunch, and dinner experiences. Their extensive menus are divided into multiple categories of small plates. Mezzes include spreads, charcuterie, and pickled vegetables, while soups and salads include veal and tomato soups and salads of greens and grains. The baked dishes category emphasizes cheese and meat pies and white and Sudzuk (a dry, spicy, fermented sausage) flatbreads. Smoked eggplant and cauliflower are among the vegetable offerings, and kebabs and skewers of lamb, chicken, and pork neck round out the grill section. A smorgasbord of slow-cooked meats like

Left: A banquet of bites awaits. *Right:* Ending on a sweet note. Photos courtesy of Tigran Markaryan of Calypso Digital Weddings and Ambar.

beef short rib goulash and lamb shoulder, as well as fish and seafood dishes including rainbow trout and drunken mussels, complement the already expansive banquet. Make sure to save room for their dessert platter composed of baklava and chocolate and raspberry cakes. The limitless menu also includes a selection of cocktails, wines, and beers. Ambar's brunch menu also features egg dishes, sliders, and sides like bacon and potato hash.

Try the regional drink Rakia, a popular fruit brandy that's traditionally served as a welcome toast among family and friends. For an additional fee, diners can choose a tasting of three Rakias from over a dozen choices.

Multiple locations
Original location: 523 8th St. SE, 202-813-3039
ambarrestaurant.com

Being a regular at Ambar has its perks! Guests have the option to enroll in Ambar's multitiered House Accounts program, where they'll earn bonus dining credits to use at the restaurant group's multiple locations and receive early access to special offers and exclusive events.

ASTRO DOUGHNUTS & FRIED CHICKEN

A mouthwatering marriage of two comfort food favorites

Has anyone ever been sad after eating a doughnut? Perhaps, but highly unlikely. Deep-fried, sugary rounds of perfection will make any day brighter; that's pretty much a guarantee. Few foods can rival fried chicken as comfort food. Sinking your teeth into succulent meat enveloped in a crispy coating is one of life's greatest joys. What's even better than savoring these two comfort food favorites individually? Indulging in a transcendental union of the two. From stuffed sensations bursting with cream to crispy, juicy pieces of tender fried chicken, Astro Doughnuts & Fried Chicken has taught us that thankfully, we don't have to choose.

Childhood friends and homegrown Washingtonians Jeff Halpern and Elliot Spaisman have shared a love for two American favorites since they were kids: ice hockey and American comfort food. They grew up playing hockey, often celebrating postgame with their favorite hockey puck–shaped confection. The duo went on to become the first native Washingtonians to play for the Washington Capitals before partnering to serve up some of the best doughnuts and fried chicken the nation's capital has to offer. Today, they have managed to feed the masses with a winning combination; anyone who didn't know they needed a doughnut–fried chicken dual concept in their life before, certainly knows now.

Astro's prized pastry crème brûlée doughnut is otherworldly, a soft, pillowy fried dough oozing with a creamy custard center jacketed with vanilla glaze and sugar brûlée. Few combinations can rival the

Left: Astro's crème brûlée doughnuts. *Right:* Astro's peanut butter and jelly doughnuts. Photos courtesy of Scott Suchman.

salty-sweet duo of peanut butter and jelly. Here, everyone's favorite childhood classic is stuffed with strawberry jam and topped with a peanut butter glaze and chopped peanuts. These dreamy doughnut doozies might just make morning people out of us after all.

For those craving something more on the savory side, Astro's serves fried chicken goodness throughout the day. Wake up to a fried egg BYO chicken sandwich, or fried chicken honey, a chicken breast smothered with honey butter and hot sauce. If you can stave off fried chicken cravings to a bit later in the day, there are plenty of lunch and dinner choices to fill your bellies and entice your taste buds. Can't decide between a doughnut or fried chicken? With Astro's Old Bay, you can have both! The miraculous marriage of the two features a fried chicken breast topped with bacon, pickles, lettuce, tomato, and Sriracha Mayo on an Old Bay Doughnut. A game-winning goal if there ever was one.

1308 G St. NW, 202-809-5565
Multiple locations in Virginia
astrodoughnuts.com

Looking to share the joy of delicious doughnuts and crispy fried chicken at your next event? Astro Doughnuts and Fried Chicken offers an extensive catering menu that will make any gathering a sweet and savory success.

YEKTA PERSIAN MARKET & KABOB COUNTER

The DMV's oldest Iranian market

Yekta Market resembles a Middle Eastern bazaar where senses are heightened and wanderlust is evoked. What's exotic to some is a source of comfort to others, and there lies the beauty of this cherished, family-run market. As the region's oldest Iranian market, Yekta has proudly served both long-time regulars and curious newcomers for over 40 years.

In 1977, Yadi Dadras and his family left Iran and immigrated to the United States. Two years later, Dadras and his uncle opened Yekta to create a space where Iranians could find the familiar foods and products of home. Meaning "unique" or "only one" in Farsi, Yekta was the area's first market of its kind. While Middle Eastern and other ethnic markets are more prevalent today, in the late 1970s there was nothing like it for miles. Dadras was a pioneer in his own right, aptly naming his market and paving the way for the many who followed.

Today sisters Sougol Mollaan and Sahel Dadras carry on the family legacy by honoring the vision of their late father. They grew up running around the market and watching their family interact with customers. Now as co-owners, they are committed to upholding family traditions while leaving their own mark. When the demand for takeout, delivery, and cooking at home increased during the pandemic, Sougul and Sahel did away with the establishment's restaurant to expand their market and add a Kabobi counter. There you can choose from a wide array of kabobs like koobideh (Persian ground meat), and joojeh (cornish hen with saffron and citrus marinade). Specialty dishes include ghormeh sabzi (slow-cooked

Left: Yekta's cornucopia of delights and kabob counter. *Right:* Yekta's shelves upon shelves of goodies. Photos courtesy of Yekta Market & Yekta Kabob Counter.

beef stew with kidney beans) and fesenjan (sweet and sour chicken stew made with pomegranate molasses and ground walnuts).

Marvel at shelves spilling over with nuts and seeds like pistachios and black lemon seeds, dried beans like fava and lentils, and noodles like vermicelli and orzo. Tantalize your taste buds with a gold mine of honeys, preserves, and jams, and wallow in sticky-sweet treats like baklava and Persian nougat. Revel in the market's cornucopia of spices and herbs, breads, fresh fruits and vegetables, and coffee and teas. Prepared and refrigerated foods including falafel mixes, dips, and dairy products are also available.

While some market aspects have evolved since patriarch Dadras opened its doors, many have remained the same. For over 40 years, customers have witnessed Sougol and Sahel growing up here while bringing their children and their children's children to the community-centric hub reminiscent of their native home.

1488 Rockville Pike, Rockville, MD
Market: 301-984-1190 | Kabob Counter: 301-984-0005
yektamarket.com

In addition to visiting Yekta's market and Kabobi counter, customers can purchase Persian and Middle Eastern grocery products from their extensive online store.

BRESCA | JÔNT

Reach for the stars and find bistronomic bliss

Three times a charm, especially when it comes to the highly coveted Michelin Star. Ryan Ratino, acclaimed chef, and owner of Bresca and Jônt restaurants, knows firsthand just how special earning three Michelin Stars is. He's been dreaming of the distinguished honor ever since his culinary school days at Le Cordon Bleu. Ratino began studying the elevated dining world, describing his love for this style of cooking as "falling in a trance," becoming obsessed with its precision, refinement, and innovation. Poring over *The French Laundry* cookbook, he strived to join the ranks of the world's greatest chefs, wanting to be elite without being elitist. As the youngest US chef to be at the helm of a two-starred restaurant, and the youngest chef ever to boast two different starred establishments, it's only fitting that his culinary school peers dubbed Ratino as "The Michelin Man."

Ratino didn't grow up in a food-centric household; he learned how to cook in hopes of helping his busy working mom. As a kid, he watched Emeril Lagasse's cooking show and began experimenting with re-creating his dishes.Later he started working in the restaurant industry, further fueling his fervor for cooking. Over the years, Ratino's zeal for food has only grown. He spends his days cooking and reading cookbooks, and he plans travels solely around researching restaurants and cocktail bars.

Ratino opened Bresca in September 2017.The 60-seat contemporary bistro focuses on Paris bistronomy, the belief that high-level cuisine can thrive in a casual and friendly environment. Ratino strongly believes that haute cuisine doesn't have to be pretentious; he and his team work hard to cultivate an inviting atmosphere where spirited conversations and unabashed laughter are encouraged. Bresca's seasonal menu illustrates

Top: Brioche stuffed chicken. Photo courtesy of Bresca. *Center:* Jônt Chef Ryan Ratino. *Bottom:* Jônt's dry-aged duck. Photos courtesy of Jônt.

its commitment to responsibly sourced ingredients, featuring the highest-quality produce, seafood, and meat available. Dishes are inspired both regionally and internationally, grounded in classic French cooking and imbued with mid-Atlantic flavors. Multi-course prix fixe menus are divided into categories including snacks; medium plates; and larger, shareable plates. Ratino's famed dry-aged duck leads the lineup of impressive and memorable dishes.

Upstairs, sister restaurant Jônt is Ratino's fine-dining tasting-counter concept. The encore establishment seats 12 to 14 guests in an intimate, wood-fired setting. Exceptional cooking techniques and top-shelf ingredients are at the core of the exquisite dining experience. The 32-course menu highlights some of the finest ingredients in the world, many procured during Ratino's frequent travels to Japan. The dishes here are flawless and the service is impeccable, creating an awe-inspiring experience from start to finish. Their beverage menu is equally extensive, including three different wine pairings, a lovely selection of teas from DC's Teaism, and a tableside presentation of traditional matcha service. While luxury and playfulness don't often go hand in hand, the talented team at Jônt does an outstanding job of creating a lavish yet affable environment.

Bresca
1906 14th St. NW
www.brescadc.com

Jônt
1904 14th St. NW, 202-518-7926
jontdc.com

PUPUSAS

The Salvadoran specialty we love to savor

Salvadorans make up the largest immigrant population in Washington, and lucky for all of us, we've been reaping the benefits of the Central American country's food and culture for years. A pupusa, El Salvador's national dish, is a masa flour pouch stuffed with savory fillings like beans, cheese, loroco flowers, or meat. Regardless of your filling of choice, curtido, a tangy Salvadoran fermented cabbage slaw, pairs perfectly with the stuffed corn cake treat. The DMV is chock-full of pupusa places that will surely warm your heart and satisfy your appetite.

Head to the highly diverse town of Wheaton for some of the best pupusas (and Latino cuisine) around. Independently owned Chorros has been a regional stalwart, serving scratch-made pupusas that are widely considered some of the area's tastiest, for over 30 years. Pedro and Reina Lazo opened the eatery in 1989, bringing 12 years of experience in the Salvadoran and Mexican food industries. They've since passed the torch to their two sons, Omar and Jason, who carry on their family tradition through their homestyle dishes. You'll have your pick of pupusas at this legendary establishment. Try the Suprema, a supersized pupusa loaded with pork, cheese, refried beans, onion, bell peppers, loroco, and jalapeño.

Popular Silver Spring staple Samantha's Restaurant serves an array of ravishing Latin American dishes including pupusas stuffed with atypical fillings like zucchini and spinach. For something different, try the pupusas mariscos (seafood).

DC's Mount Pleasant and Columbia Heights enclaves are home to a large Latino population. Start your pupusa tour at neighborhood fixture Don Juan. The colorful establishment offers a long menu of

Left: Gloria's Pupuseria. *Center:* Cheese and bean pupusa at Don Juan. *Right:* Pupusa with curtido. Photo courtesy of Peter Fitzgerald, Wikimedia Commons.

Salvadoran and Mexican dishes, including warm and hearty made-to-order pupusas. Don't miss tiny-but-mighty Gloria Pupuseria, a no-frills joint cooking up made-to-order pupusas that are hot, crisp, and brimming with all the mouthwatering fillings you came for: cheese, beans, and/or pork. The stuffed sensations are accompanied by black beans, pickled cabbage, and red salsa.

Named for a little plaza located near an active volcano in San Miguel, El Salvador, Las Placitas was founded by brothers Isidoro, Ramon, and Jose Amaya in 1990. Their lengthy menu emphasizes Salvadoran and Mexican cuisines, including pupusas, enchiladas, fajitas, and chimichangas.

What's just as fantastic as these bundles of belly-warming goodness? The price! Most of these pupusas range between $1.75 and $3.99, making them an equally affordable and luscious treat.

Los Chorros
2420 Blueridge Ave., Wheaton, MD
301-933-1066
loschorrosrestaurant.com

Samantha's Restaurant
631 University Blvd. E
Silver Spring, MD, 301-445-7300
samanthasrestaurante.com

Don Juan Restaurant
1660 Lamont St. NW, 202-667-0010

Gloria's Pupuseria
3411 14th St. NW, 202-884-0105

Las Placitas
1100 8th St. SE, 202-543-3700
lasplacitasrestaurant.com

STICKY FINGERS BAKERY & DINER

Plant-based goodness proving there's no butter way to eat and bake a mess

Growing up in an Italian-Jewish family, Doron Petersan was accustomed to the foods of her two ancestries being intermingled, or as the Sticky Fingers founder describes, "smashed" together. Eating often involved intertwining Jewish delicacies like bagels and knishes with Italian cookies and breads. Doron's most indelible memories revolve around the holidays, when Doron could indulge in her favorite foods. When Doron went vegan in her early 20s, she didn't want to sacrifice the foods that she had loved growing up. Plant-based products and ingredients were scarce at the time, so Doron re-created her own childhood favorites. This time they'd be plant-based, but in no way less delicious.

Doron studied food and nutrition, but it was a food science class that left the greatest impression on the two-time *Cupcake Wars* winner and cookbook author. She was intrigued by the science behind food and the impact it can have upon health, and also by the chemistry involved in producing and deconstructing something irresistible. Doron made candy and cakes at home, experimenting with different techniques and high temperatures. Her talents attracted attention, and when people began offering to pay for her desserts, she seized the opportunity.

Doron can't help but laugh when thinking about the business plan she drew up with a pencil and a sheet of paper. While her initial plan may have needed some tweaking, her brilliance and resourcefulness in the kitchen did not. Doron found a space in Dupont Circle, searched high and low for plant-based ingredients, and whisked up

Left: Sticky buns. *Top center:* Cocktails upon cocktails. *Above center:* Garlic and onion potato pierogies with sauerkraut and sour cream. *Right:* Assorted cupcakes. Photos courtesy of Sticky Fingers Diner.

heavenly batches of yumminess like sticky buns and cheesecakes. A friend's documentary film about Doron's baking magic put her on the map—the world map, in fact. A Korean company licensed Sticky Fingers and brought its recipes to Seoul, where they sold the vegan confections in kiosks across the city.

Doron founded Sticky Fingers in 2002 and has been turning out sugary and savory splendidness ever since. Customers swoon over sweet-studded sensations like her Cowvin Cookies (oatmeal cookies filled with vanilla buttercream) and Fudgetastic Brownies. Ask Doron to declare her favorite cookie and she unequivocally names the Rainbow Cookie, the fought-over almond-flavored cookie slathered with the raspberry-apricot jam of her childhood. Notables like burgers, perogies, and pancakes help keep the H Street diner packed, and showstoppers like plant-based charcuterie and cashew-almond house-made burrata provide sublime and compassionate alternatives to animal meat without sacrificing one ounce of taste.

The gifted vegan baker, chef, and restaurateur proves that there's really no butter way to eat.

406 H St. NE, 202-367-9600
314 Carroll St. NW, 202-299-9700
stickyfingersdiner.com

CAPITOL HILL CULINARY CORNERS

Hollis Silverman and Micheline Mendelsohn cultivate nourishing spaces for the community

In a neighborhood often marred by clashing political powers, two Capitol Hill culinary corners stand out, providing cherished havens for the community to gather and eat.

Hollis Silverman partitioned her 8,400-square-foot corner into three distinctive spaces: one reflecting the food of her New England childhood and time lived in California (The Duck & the Peach), another where families and friends could gather (La Collina), and a cocktail bar reminiscent of the lively gin joints she frequented while traveling through Spain (The Wells). Silverman has spent most of her distinguished career working to improve the restaurant industry and its devoted workforce. She fervently believes that food is as much medicine as it is nourishment, and has scrupulously curated menus centered on natural, organic, and locally sourced ingredients. Begin your meal at the Duck & the Peach with in-house-baked Parker House rolls slathered with almond dukkah goat butter. Bask in the bounty of garden vegetables like grilled ramps and feast on the restaurant's namesake, the rotisserie pekin duck with citrus vinaigrette. At La Collina (Italian for "hill") pastas are made in-house, and delights like burrata and arancini kick off a superb lineup. Kids will enjoy elevated but approachable classics like fusilli and spaghetti and meatballs. Next door, step into The Wells, a sleek gin bar where tones of forest green and copper lend to its luxuriously intriguing vibe. Gin shines brightly here in its grand mix of floral and herbaceous cocktails.

A few blocks away stands another revered nook operated by the Mendelsohn family, the owners behind six restaurant concepts.

Top: La Collina, a neighborhood gem. Photo courtesy of Louis Tinsley. *Bottom:* The Mendelsohn Family. Photo courtesy of Joe Shymanski.

Coming on the heels of Chef Spike's success on *Top Chef,* the Mendelsohns struck while the iron was hot, opening Good Stuff Eatery in 2008. From its inception, the casual joint has attracted a devout following with their gourmet burgers, hand-spun milkshakes, and hand-cut fries. Several years later, We, The Pizza opened next door, followed by neighboring Santa Rosa Taqueria, further cementing the family's stronghold in the community. Recipes across restaurant concepts are designed to elicit feelings of comfort and nostalgia with a twist. Over 15 years later, the tight-knit family of four continues to draw upon each member's area of expertise and has built an international empire. From the DMV to Cairo, Micheline Mendelsohn, deputy chief executive director, and team continue to seek out challenges, describing their expansion as leaving a little mark of Americana wherever they go.

The Duck & the Peach
300 7th St. SE,
202-431-1913
duckandpeachdc.com

La Collina
747 C St. SE,
202-998-2799
lacollinadc.com

The Wells
727 C St. SE
thewellsdc.com

Méli Wine and Mezze
1630 Columbia Rd. NW,
202-978-2333
melidc.com

Good Stuff Eatery
Multiple locations
Flagship: 303
Pennsylvania Ave. SE
202-791-0168
goodstuffeatery.com

We, The Pizza
Multiple locations
303 Pennsylvania Ave. SE
202-544-4008
wethepizza.com

Santa Rosa Taqueria
301 Pennsylvania Ave.
SE, 202-450-4800
santarosataqueria.com

EDEN CENTER & RICE PAPER

A Vietnamese cultural and culinary epicenter

Recognized as the largest Vietnamese commercial and cultural center on the East Coast, Eden Center is an epicenter for authentic Vietnamese food, specialties, and services. Since 1984 the institution has been home to nearly 120 family-owned establishments, including restaurants, bakeries, supermarkets, and cafés.

Eden Center was established in hopes of reviving Clarendon's once-prosperous Vietnamese neighborhood, Little Saigon. From the mid-1970s to the mid-'80s, the lost enclave of Little Saigon was a haven for Vietnamese refugees who had fled their homes after the fall of Saigon in 1975. Many escaped to Arlington due to its proximity to US government agencies as well as its established community of recent immigrants.

Rice Paper owner Mai Lam came to Arlington with her family when she was five years old. Her father worked as a goldsmith, eventually opening a jewelry store in Eden Center, where they would become a pillar for the next 27 years. After their father's death, Mai, along with her mother, Xuan Tran, and cousin Phuong Ho, reassessed the family business and decided to change course. They drew upon their unparalleled cooking skills, strong business acumen, and eternal love for their homeland to open a restaurant. They were united in their vision: cooking authentic Vietnamese food for everyone, regardless of age, background, or heritage. Their homestyle cooking is designed to elicit memories of a distant home for some, while introducing others to the flavors and culture of Vietnam.

The family matriarch and long-standing chef has since packed up her kitchen tools, but Xuan Tran continues to be involved in many of the restaurant's operations. Mai and Phuong have carried the

Left: Chim cút quay (marinated quail). Photo courtesy of Rice Paper. *Top right:* Eden Center shines a bright light on Vietnamese culture and food. Photo courtesy of Mdy66, Wikimedia Commons. *Above right:* Stuffed, rolled, and ready to be enjoyed. Photo courtesy of Rice Paper.

family torch, creating a dynamic range of dishes that honor their mother's recipes while adding purposeful touches of modernity. Mai describes a typical Vietnamese family meal as consisting of steamed rice, a small portion of animal protein, herbaceous leafy greens, and accompanying dipping sauces and herbs. Vietnamese food is often characterized by its light flavors, often void of dairy, heavy oil, and added sugars. Lush green herbs like cilantro and basil add freshness and brightness to most dishes.

With a menu boasting nearly 100 dishes, there's no shortage of delights to savor and slurp. Customer favorites include Cơm Tấm Đặc Biệt (a rice platter stacked with grilled pork chop, tofu stuffed with shrimp paste, shrimp, fried egg, shredded pork, and shrimp rolls) and bánh xèo (a crepe stuffed with shrimp, pork, mung beans, onions, and bean sprouts).

Eden Center
6751–6799 Wilson Blvd.
Falls Church, VA
info@edencenter.com
edencenter.com

Rice Paper
6775 Wilson Blvd., Falls Church, VA
703-538-3888
ricepaper-tasteofvietnam.com

PRESCRIPTION CHICKEN

Rx for the soup-loving soul

After a bout with laryngitis and an unsuccessful late-night search for homemade chicken noodle soup, Val Zweig decided to take matters into her own hands. She enlisted her cousin Taryn Pellicone, and together the two "chix," as they cleverly call themselves, teamed up to create homemade chicken noodle soup that would alter DC's soup scene forever.

Val and Taryn began cooking in Val's kitchen, simmering steaming batches of grandma-style chicken noodle and matzah ball soup. They eventually took their skills to Mess Hall, where they joined fellow cooks in the shared commercial kitchen space. Here, the duo had immediate access to cookware, appliances, and a wealth of other benefits within the food and beverage community. They launched their delivery service in 2016, using increasingly popular delivery platforms like Uber Eats to expand their reach across the region. Soon their soothing soups found their way into countless homes, helping alleviate common colds and debilitating hangovers while providing flavorsome tastes of home.

From the beginning, Val and Taryn have stayed true to their core beliefs and product. While they have added to their soup repertoire, they have chosen to remain focused on what they know and do best: cooking up belly-warming, soul-satisfying soup. Soup selections include Chickenless/Vegetarian, Pho-in-One, Ramen-ish, and Bi-

> Flavorful feel-good food is meant to be shared! Prescription Chicken offers mail-order packages including the Super Sick Package, the Ultimate Hangover Package, the New Mama Package, and the Destress Package.

Left: Matzah ball soup. Photo courtesy of Mango Tomato. *Center:* Prescription Chicken cofounders Val Zweig (left) and Taryn Pellicone (right). Photo courtesy of Prescription Chicken. *Right:* Chicken soup is good for the soul. Photo courtesy of Mango Tomato.

partisan Chicken Soup, a marriage of their OG classics: matzah balls and egg noodles. They're confident in their product and recognize the limitless opportunities surrounding it. As the chix explain, there is no need to do a thousand different things when they can successfully do a thousand things within their core concept.

Noticing a glaring lack of local soups in grocery stores, the pair launched their grocery retail line, Chix Soup Co, in 2016, which made its debut at Glen's Garden Market. Today their soups can be found in 650 grocery stores nationwide ranging from smaller markets like Yes! Organic Market to national heavy hitters like Costco.

The powerhouse pair eventually left the shared kitchen space and moved into a brick-and-mortar in Shaw. The shared concept remains important to them, and they co-occupy the space with Doro Soul Food and Motown Square Pizza.

While talent, grit, and dedication to their craft have been integral factors in their success, Val and Taryn also attribute their accomplishments to the tight-knit food community around them. So many supported the twosome along their journey, and they pride themselves in being able to pay it forward any chance they get.

Prescription Chicken
1819 7th St. NW, 202-262-3235
prescriptionchicken.com

Mess Hall
703 Edgewood St. NE
messhalldc.com

CAUSA | AMAZONIA

Peruvian cuisine done two delectable ways

While DC's Latin communities have helped shape the area's diverse dining scene, Peruvian cuisine, particularly *upscale* Peruvian cuisine, has been underrepresented for some time. Chef Carlos Delgado and Service Bar owners Chad Spangler and Glendon Hartley have made it their mission to change that, taking on the roles of ambassadors of Peruvian cuisine and culture. With their stunning two-level operation of Causa and Amazonia, they've introduced diners to the cuisine's other side, illuminating its complexities, richness, and distinctiveness. The illustrious trio hopes to shake the "mom and pop" stigma and demonstrate just how refined Peruvian food can be. In undertaking this mission they have added a burst of flavor to DC's dining landscape, proving that Peruvian fare extends far beyond popular standbys like pisco sours and lomo saltado.

Chef Carlos Delgado grew up in the Peruvian seaside city of Callo cooking with his grandmother and working in restaurants. He immigrated to the US with his mother when he was 12 and continued to cook the dishes of his homeland. His stellar résumé includes being the owner and chef of shuttered Ocopa and executive chef of José Andrés's China Chilcano. When Delgado, Spangler, and Hartley embarked upon their venture, they traveled to Peru several times to research and fully immerse themselves in the culture.

Causa and Amazonia celebrate the nation's cultural diversity, wealth of ingredients, and varied topography. Dishes reflect the country's three distinct geographical regions: the decorated Pacific coastline, remote Amazon rainforest, and the Andes Mountains. The imposing establishment is a kaleidoscope of hues, exploding with a

Left: Go fish and taste something delicious. *Right:* It's all in the name. Photos courtesy of Rey Lopez.

vibrant jungle of greenery, an airy rooftop bar, and a swanky lounge to see and be seen in.

Occupying the first floor is the intimate luminous dining room Causa. The meticulously crafted six-course tasting menu leads diners through a tantalizing tour of Peruvian coastal and Andes fare. Here, seafood and fish from their fish market are emphasized.

Upstairs is their more casual and buzzing concept, Amazonia. Shareable plates reflect the flavors of the Peruvian rainforest. The à la carte menu is divided into categories: snacks, la anticucheria (skewers of shrimp, salmon belly, etc.), cold and hot dishes, and desserts. Highlights include cebiche Amazonia, pulpo al olivo, and arroz con erizos a la chiclayana (a rice dish brimming with delights like sea urchin, kabocha, and bomba).

Causa's glowing success received further recognition when Washington's Michelin Guide added the restaurant to their lauded list in March 2023.

920 Blagden Alley
Blagden Alley is located between 9th and 10th Streets NW
or M and N Streets NW, 202-629-3942
causadc.com

*Please note: There is only pedestrian traffic in the alley;
vehicular traffic is not permitted.*

MAMBO SAUCE

Sauce imitates politics: DC's sweet and spicy controversial sauce

In a political city frequently plagued by controversy, it's only fitting that its most treasured sauce should follow suit. That's right, even Mambo sauce, DC's favorite red-orange sweet-and-tangy sauce, carries a bit of the baggage often affiliated with our capital city.

While the most fanatic Washingtonians insist that Mambo sauce is a homegrown Washington wonder, the truth is that DC's most prized condiment isn't from DC after all. No, in fact, it originated in Chicago. That's right. In 2013 a judge ruled that "mumbo," one of many of the sauce's alternative spellings, is legally trademarked in Chicago, where some argue the sauce was first created in the 1950s by Argia B. Collins, an African American restaurateur. Enter Arsha Jones, CEO and founder of Capital City Mambo Sauce. Jones filed a petition to cancel the trademark, noting that "mumbo sauce" is simply the name for a carryout sauce, not a specific one. The judge didn't see it that way, but Jones was undeterred. The DC native started her Mambo sauce business with her late husband after moving to the suburbs and missing the beloved sauce she grew up with. She took the sauce that she regularly cooked for her family and decided to broaden its scope, selling it to the masses. Jones's homestyle Mambo sauce has grown into a regional phenomenon, sold in many major local grocery stores, Eastern and Union Markets, and Ben's Chili Bowl Gift Shop.

The sweet-and-spicy sensation is redolent of Chinese sweet-and-sour sauce mixed with ketchup. It's a perfect complement to fried chicken wings, fried rice, french fries, and just about any other guilty pleasure you can think of. A whole slew of eateries, particularly

110

Left: Capital City's founder and CEO, Arsha Jones. *Right:* Wings and Capital City Mambo Sauce—a match made in heaven. Photos courtesy of Capital City.

fried fast-food joints, carry Washington's crowned jewel. One of the District's go-to spots for Mambo sauce is Yum's II Carryout, which specializes in Americanized Chinese food. Mambo enthusiasts flock to Yum's for their jumbo wings topped with their own spin on the famed sauce. Over on U Street, soul-food legend Henry's Soul Cafe's mumbo sauce pairs beautifully with their succulent fried chicken wings. Get ready to catch some heat with Wingo's special spicy mumbo sauce, guaranteed to light a fire in your belly and in your mouth! A favorite for Korean-style wings, KoChix's soy garlic and hot honey spicy mumbo sauces will leave your taste buds singing and your lips smiling.

Capital City Mambo Sauce
info@capitalcity.com
capitalcity.com

Henry's Soul Cafe
1704 U St. NW, 202-265-3336
www.henryssoulcafe.com

Yum's II Carryout
1413 14th St. NW, 202-232-5608

Wingo's
2218 Wisconsin Ave. NW
202-878-6576
wingos.com

KoChix
400 Florida Ave. NW, 202-232-3468
kochixdc.com

Z&Z MANOUSHE BAKERY

Meet the za'atar family: the manoushe masterminds of the DMV

At the front of Z&Z Manoushe Bakery sits an old Hobart mixer, a reminder of the breads the family-owned business's grandmother used to bake. The prized heirloom serves as a symbol of the food and culture that have helped shape the family for over 40 years.

In the 1980s, cofounders Danny and Johnny Dubbaneh's father and grandfather immigrated to the US from Palestine and Jordan. While they ran fried chicken and sub shops, at home they cooked the foods of their Arabic heritage. As kids, the brothers were painstakingly aware of how different their packed lunches were compared to the Lunchables of their peers. With age, they learned to appreciate Arabic food, wanting to hold onto their cultural identity as much as possible. While their parents had hoped they would choose careers far away from the restaurant industry, entrepreneurship was in their blood, steering them to follow in their family's footsteps. Their love language has always been food. It's how their family shows love and takes care of each other, and they wanted to share that with others. In 2016, the brothers left their corporate careers and set out to make manoushe, the popular Palestinian street snack of their childhood and emblem of their heritage.

They launched their new venture at a Foggy Bottom farmers market, selling warm and crispy flatbread slathered with olive oil and za'atar to an instantly loyal following. As their popularity grew, so did their presence, as they soon added multiple markets to their expanding business. They cherished the community connections they helped foster, and they longed to re-create that sense of kinship in a more permanent space. On a whim, they contacted the owner of their grandfather's former fried chicken shop, asking if she was

Left: Za'atar spice mix. Photo courtesy of Deb Lindzey. *Center:* Brothers and cofounders Danny (left) and Johnny (right) Dubbaneh. *Right:* Manoushe Lebanese Bride (left), Toum Raider (center), and Jibneh (right). Photos courtesy of Z&Z.

interested in selling. As fate would have it, she was looking to retire, so they secretly purchased it, surprising their family with the return of the business. During renovations, they discovered their grandfather's writing adorning the walls and even uncovered a lost family photo buried under three layers of tile from 25 years ago.

Today you'll find throngs of people lining up for their manoushe fresh out of the wood-fired oven. Traditionists may gravitate toward the za'atar, while more adventurous palates have their choice of interesting toppings like sujuk (beef sausage), pickled turnips, Arab pickles, and cheeses. Can't decide? Order a few extra to bring home and discover just how rewarding a fridge stocked with leftovers can be.

1111 Nelson St., Rockville, MD, 301-296-4178
zandzdc.com

From farmers markets to grocery shelves to the freezer aisle: Z&Z products, including their renowned manoushe, za'atar, and sumac spices, are available in dozens of DMV-area grocery stores like Whole Foods, Mom's Organic, and Dawson's Market, as well as in some select stores in Pennsylvania, New Jersey, New York, and Massachusetts.

LAOS IN TOWN

Laotian fare in the heart of NoMa

Ben Tiatasin may have grown up cooking Thai food, but her true love is Laotian cuisine. She credits her grandmother for her ardor for cooking, having developed an affinity for Southeast Asian cuisine at a young age. Ben began traveling to Laos as a teenager and was enamored with its food's vibrancy and freshness. While Thai and Laotian cuisines share commonalities, there are distinct differences. Laotian food is typically lighter, packed with herbs and chilies, while Thai food is often richer and creamier. Thai dishes are typically served individually, while Laotian food is intended to be shared.

Arriving in the US in 2012, Ben drew on her travels to cook at several restaurants. She immersed herself in kitchens and experimented with the cooking methods she learned during her trips. To truly experience Laotian food, Ben emphasizes the necessity of leaving the big cities and venturing out to the countryside. Month-long homestays allowed Ben to learn authentic techniques that she would ultimately bring back to her own restaurant kitchens.

As the executive chef of Laos in Town, Ben is involved in every aspect of its menu. Seasonality and availability of ingredients play a significant role. During winter months Ben focuses on comforting dishes like noodle soups, and during the summer her dishes reflect lighter flavors. The talented chef enjoys working with a myriad of

---

Leave room for dessert! Visit the bakery and indulge in Chef Tiatasin's cake table, where cakes are made daily. Craving even more sweetness in your life? Their mango pandan sticky rice has been a crowd-pleaser for years.

Top: LaoWok Noodles. Center: Grilled chicken heart. Bottom: Herbal sausage. Photos courtesy of Rey Lopez.

spices and ingredients, her favorite being the kaffir leaf because of its aromatic qualities and spiced-citrus flavor. Ben visits Laos annually in search of inspiration and knowledge, and to bring back indigenous ingredients that are unavailable in the States. A lifelong student, Ben's committed to continuously refining her craft and evolving as a chef.

Multiple dishes help define Laos in Town. Mieng kana, a lettuce wrap filled with Chinese broccoli, vermicelli noodles, and shrimp, is Ben's fresh take on the popular delicacy. Grilled chicken heart, a Laotian staple, is difficult to track down here, but for the tenacious chef, the search is nearly as satisfying as the creation. The grilled chicken, a whole Cornish hen seasoned with roasted rice powder and sweet sauces, has been on the menu since the beginning. Pla tong na, the eatery's most popular dish, stars a crispy rockfish layered with spices like chili, lemongrass, and ginger.

Whether you're new to Laotian food or you've been savoring it for years, you'll find dishes and ingredients here that are rarely found elsewhere. Chef Ben Tiatasin guarantees it.

250 K St. NE, 202-864-6687
laosintown.com

PLEASE BRING CHIPS

A place where deliciousness and ingenuity keep popping up

Is it a pop-up place? A catering venue? An event space? A spot where ingenious individuals join forces to support and elevate fellow food and beverage enthusiasts? A resounding *yes* to all the above. But wait, there's more! Please Bring Chips is changing how we think about eating and drinking, so while you're not actually required to bring any chips, you do need to bring your appetite and enthusiasm for the unconventional experience that's about to ensue.

Cofounder and managing partner Chad Drummond has always been passionate about food and drink. While his friends were drinking Natty Light in college, Chad was researching German lagers and ales. In 2015, he collaborated with No Kings Collective, a local creative energy space specializing in public art installations, to bartend a New Year's Eve pop-up soiree. As Chad began building his team, he created spreadsheets to stay organized. Over time, he and his team became savvier and their events became more polished and refined. Chad's early spreadsheets were soon replaced by complex systems and sophisticated algorithms designed to collect data to help scale up for large events. While their initial concept has grown exponentially, their mindset has remained unchanged. Every element of Please Bring Chips is deliberate, with an unrelenting emphasis on its team and cultivating partnerships both internationally and with local makers and food and beverage entities.

Please Bring Chips left culinary incubator Mess Hall to move into the shuttered Thamee's space on H Street NE. They designated upstairs as a pop-up area where they could support local businesses and industry friends as well as take risks and challenge the status quo of traditional entertaining. Their first pop-up spotlighted uber-talented Magpie and

Top left: The Incredible Team at Fray-On-Tap Event. Photo courtesy of Please Bring Chips *Above left:* Deliciousness Pairs Beautifully with a Martini. *Top right:* Sipsational Cocktails at Shababi's Pop-Up Event. Photos courtesy of Farrah Skeiky. *Above right:* Fridays and Cocktails at the Freer. Photo courtesy of Please Bring Chips.

the Tiger, followed by subsequent pop-ups that have included Shababi Palestinian Chicken, Ek' Balam, a Riviera Maya–inspired culinary adventure; and Fruits and Flowers, a sensory wine experience. Don't be surprised if a non-food-and-drink experience pops up; remember, there are no rules here. The ever-evolving space has also teamed up with multidisciplinary creative studio Studio Sonic to host a clothing pop-up.

When Chad describes what he is most proud of, neither the emblazoned growth nor the epic success surrounding Please Bring Chips is mentioned. Rather, he fondly references the team's diversity and shared vision, and let's not forget the utter brilliance required for creating transformative and unforgettable experiences night after night, event after incredible event.

1320 H St. NE, hey@pleasebringchips.com
pleasebringchips.com

Beyond Please Bring Chips's unique pop-ups, they cater large events and festivals and also offer cocktail classes, all with garnishes of edge and ingenuity.

MARTIN'S TAVERN

A presidential affair

As a beloved Georgetown institution since 1933, Martin's Tavern is the community's oldest family-run restaurant. Its old-DC charm and convivial ambience have been welcoming patrons for nearly a century. Its allure, however, transcends its food and neighborhood-friendly approach. The main draw here is its remarkable history; Martin's has proudly hosted every US president from Harry S. Truman to George W. Bush. While seated at one of Martin's wooden booths, you may find yourself sitting among the soon-to-be-presidents who have dined here as congressmen, governors, senators, and CIA directors.

It's easy to spot where future commanders in chief sat as plaques above booths and tables mark their favorite spots within the tavern. Booth #1, also known as the "Rumble Seat," is where John F. Kennedy read his Sunday morning paper after Mass at Holy Trinity each week. It's also at this booth where Kennedy drafted his inauguration speech following the 1960 presidential election. Richard Nixon frequently dined at Martin's throughout the 1940s and 1950s as a representative, senator, and vice president. The "Nixon Booth" (Booth #2) commemorates Nixon's time here; he was often accompanied by fellow congressional colleagues and was known to enjoy Martin's famous Grandma Martin's Meatloaf. Harry and Bess Truman dined in Booth #6 with their daughter, Margaret,

> Brunch lovers don't have to wait for the weekend to enjoy one of DC's favorite pastimes. Martin's serves brunch every day until 4:00 p.m. Brunch offerings include steak and eggs, Martin's Chesapeake Benedict, challah French toast, and Martin's Biscuits and Gravy.

Top: Bottom line—the cocktails at Martin's are delicious. *Center:* Welcome to Martin's. *Bottom:* Brunch at Martin's Tavern. Photos courtesy of Martin's Tavern.

while she was attending George Washington University. Margaret later incorporated Martin's into her mystery novels. Lyndon Baines Johnson often dined with former Speaker of the House Sam Rayburn in Booth #24, now known as the "LBJ Booth." George W. Bush and his family sat at Table 12 while visiting then President George H. Bush and First Lady Barbara Bush.

Undeniably, the tavern's most famous booth is Booth #3, proving that romance is far from being dead. It's here that then-Senator John F. Kennedy proposed to his girlfriend Jacqueline Lee Bouvier on June 24, 1953. Although the engagement took place in a public setting, the event was a quiet one, absent of any grand gestures, words, or bended knee. The booth has since been dubbed the "The Proposal Booth," with many other couples following suit by getting engaged in this historic booth.

Martin's prides itself on being a family-operated restaurant and its menu reflects the kind of comfort fare one might enjoy at a family dinner. Guest favorites include the traditional oyster stew and Martin's Delight, Martin's version of the hot brown: sliced turkey over toast smothered in homemade rarebit sauce broiled in a cast-iron skillet.

1264 Wisconsin Ave. NW, 202-333-7370
martinstavern.com

BRONZE

Afrofuturism-inspired merging of science fiction, food, and the culture of the African Diaspora

Bronze and its Afrofuturism restaurant concept is the brainchild of entrepreneur and visionary Keem Hughley, a DC native who grew up just a few blocks away. Hughley's drive, along with his breadth of experience in the hospitality industry, helped pave the way for a prolific array of career endeavors, including working with distinguished chef and restaurateur Eric Bruner-Yang. Like countless others during the COVID-19 pandemic, Hughley found himself with extra time on his hands and in need of a creative outlet. He fused the history of his ancestors with a reimagining of history where freedom and unlimited opportunities existed for Black people. The remarkable result is Alonzo Bronze, a fictional traveler who serves as a medium through which Hughley tells his story.

The story of Alonzo Bronze spans 700 years and depicts the journey of a seeker and a wanderer who traveled the world to discover new cultures to learn from and share with. Hughley has centered his restaurant around Bronze and the genre of Afrofuturism, a cultural movement melding science fiction with technology, literature, music, and visual arts that puts Black history and culture at the forefront. Bronze reconceptualizes a history where Black people moved across the world to locales like the Caribbean and Brazil of their own volition, rather than being forcibly brought there. Hughley's mythical character could have never existed based on the harsh realities of the world over the past 700 years. His restaurant and menu are a bold culmination of what *could have been* if the last seven centuries had been vastly different.

Bronze's menu reflects creativity and freedom from historical constraints. Hughley, along with renowned Executive Chef Toya

Left: Bronze owner and CEO, Keem Hughley. *Center left:* Braised oxtail with papparadelle. *Center right:* Shaking things up at Bronze. *Right:* Torched oysters. Photos courtesy of Alex Clirror.

Henry, are adamant about grounding Bronze's dishes in Caribbean and Afro-Caribbean flavors; at the same time, they choose to not be beholden to specific ingredients or dishes simply because "that's how it's always been done." Instead, they've embraced this enhanced level of freedom to expand beyond the status quo. Dishes reflect their ancestors' history and culture while also employing innovative cooking techniques and emphasizing high-quality, nontraditional ingredients like yuzu and aromatics. Menu marvels include torched oysters, grilled sea bass prepared alongside green papaya and rainbow carrots, and sweet plantains accompanied by spiced crème fraîche. The restaurant's most popular dish, braised oxtail with pappardelle, is a supernova among a galaxy of gastronomic stars.

1245 H St. NE, 202-478-6833
bronzedc.com

Bronze's three-level, 5,300-square-foot space is a vision to be seen and explored as it takes diners on a voyage through multiple worlds. The sultry first-floor dining room and bar is named "pre-earth"; the second-floor dining space is dubbed "earth" and showcases stunning portraits by Nigerian artist Alibi; finally, the top floor is known as the Crane Room, a "celestial" cocktail bar highlighting mostly raw bar dishes.

MITSITAM NATIVE FOODS CAFE

Native American dishes turn the National Mall into a memorable dining destination

Widely regarded as one of America's most prized treasures, the National Mall is known for its abundance of majestic monuments and memorials, world-class museums, and thought-provoking art installations that contribute to the fabric of our capital city and country. Visitors come from near and far to meander the historical timeline of institutions lining the landscaped park, nicknamed by many "America's Front Yard." Few, however, think of the National Mall as a dining destination. Situated among an uninspiring sea of museum cafés that include fast-food joints and cafeterias, Mitsitam Cafe is a welcome reprieve for anyone seeking a unique dining experience that rises above the typical museum eatery.

Consistently voted the best Smithsonian restaurant, Mitsitam Native Foods Cafe in the National Museum of the American Indian showcases distinctive dishes and indigenous ingredients spanning the Western Hemisphere. The café's offerings are dispersed throughout five interactive food stations, each serving indigenous foods representing tribes of the Northern Woodlands, Great Plains, Northwest Coast, Mesoamerica, and South America.

Kick off your culinary trek with an appetizer like hot smoked whitefish accentuated by wild onion confit and corn relish, or try the café's totopos, corn tortillas that have been toasted, fried, or baked. One standout highlights goat, plantain and poblano salsa, and prickly pear mole served with blue, red, and yellow corn chips. A variety of soups like smoked turkey and kale garnished with turkey

Left: Inside the bright and airy café. *Center:* Making tamales. *Right:* Wild rice and watercress salad. Photos courtesy of Restaurant Associates.

chicorons served alongside a pulled buffalo sandwich with chayote squash slaw make for a satisfying lunch. Those looking for a hearty meal may want to surrender their taste buds to one of Mitsitam's bevy of burgers, including the house-ground buffalo and duck patty topped with roasted pepper dijonnaise, smoked tomatoes, and aged cheddar cheese. The eatery offers a broad selection of main dishes like grilled bison loin; roasted portobello mushroom and summer squash tostada; and Indian fry-bread tacos loaded with buffalo chili with pickled chiles and pinto beans, tomato, and shredded cheese.

Because museum-hopping can be equally enlightening and exhausting, visitors may choose to fill their bellies and stave off hunger with Mitsitam's Five Region Sampler platter, a delightful display of grilled bison striploin, cedar-planked salmon, and three regional side dishes. Sweets like strawberry rhubarb pudding, apple crumble, dried fruit bread pudding, seasonal fruit tarts, and steamed banana cake wrapped in banana leaves drizzled with blackberry sauce add a sweet finishing touch to a memorable museum meal.

Inside the National Museum of the American Indian
4th St. SW, Independence Ave. SW, 202-633-1000
mitsitamcafe.com

CHLOE

Elevated cuisine feeding the energy of the neighborhood

Chloe chef and owner Haidar Karoum has known he's wanted to be a chef since he was 12. He attributes his love for cooking to his father, a biochemist who enjoys experimenting with ingredients. Chef Karoum's cooking style is the product of his extensive travels, his Northern Irish and Lebanese ancestry, and how he prefers to eat.

Nestled into the lively Navy Yard district, Chloe strikes the perfect balance between refined cooking and approachability. Its concept is largely based upon the neighborhood haunts that Karoum has gravitated to, including favorites like San Francisco's revered Zuni Café and the late DC legend, Palena. He's an ardent believer that a dining space should feel comfortable without strict adherence to proper etiquette. Navy Yard embodies the energy that Karoum craves. As he happily shares, the neighborhood's countless dogs wagging their tails nearby serves as the perfect barometer for the enthusiasm that he seeks both inside and outside his doors.

Chef Karoum's diverse cooking career began at Michel Richard's Citronelle, followed by stints at Restaurant Nora, where he served as the Chef de Cuisine, and Asia Nora, where he "cut his teeth" and truly developed as a chef. Karoum then partnered with the late Mark Kuller and was able to home in on a variety of cuisines like Spanish at Estadio, and Thai and Vietnamese at Doi Moi.

Chloe opened in January 2018 with an eclectic menu that reflects Chef Karoum's upbringing, his travels, and the culinary education he received along the way. Kick off your meal with the fresh ricotta, a delicate plate of grilled house-made bread topped with strawberries, pickled rhubarb, and raw honey. Vegetables shine brightly here; the

Left: Chloe owner and chef Haidar Karoum. Photo courtesy of Ji Cha. *Center:* Crispy whole fish. *Right:* Hamachi crudo. Photos courtesy of Scott Suchman.

caramelized cauliflower seasoned with notes of tahini and lemon is a nod to the potluck dish Karoum's father would often bring to gatherings. It's easily one of the chef's favorites, so there's no chance of it disappearing anytime soon. The signature spiced roasted chicken is another favorite, and often Karoum's meal of choice when working in his office. Its Peking duck-like preparation involves brining with Vietnamese flavors for several hours, followed by air drying for 24 hours, and then roasting at extremely high temperatures. Preparations of menu items like the potato gnocchi dish may change slightly based on seasonality, but by and large these staples are likely here to stay. Having trouble deciding? There's no need to limit yourself; Karoum's carefully crafted plates are meant to be shared and enjoyed among company.

1331 4th St. SE, 202-313-7007
restaurantchloe.com

In addition to nightly dinner service, Chloe is open for brunch on Saturdays and Sundays. Chloe hosts private lunches for 10 to 60 people Monday through Friday. Visit their website for bookings.

UNION MARKET

The state of the union is delicious

In 2012, Union Market opened its highly anticipated food hall to colossal fanfare. As a mecca for foodies and local merchants as well as hipsters who have moved into the rejuvenated region, the feasting ground has emerged as one of the city's premier destinations. Today, more than 35 food and drink purveyors and independent business owners call the market home.

The moment I meet DC Dosa founder Priya Ammu, she envelops me in an embrace and invites me to share a meal and wine. It's clear that Ammu is someone who approaches life with warmth and zeal, just as she does in her kitchen. A native of Bombay, Ammu's affection for food began at a young age. She came to the US at 19 to attend college, later settling in DC. Her mother-in-law introduced her to dosas, crispy lentil-flour crepes stuffed with various fillings and toppings. She fell in love with the popular South Indian street food, bought herself a pressure cooker and tava (griddle), and began cooking dosas and making chutneys. Ammu tried her hand at catering and farmers markets, but it was winning a contest through Think Local First that ultimately propelled her to officially launch her business. Ammu prepares her food for her customers as she does for her family: with fresh and healthy ingredients and an abundance of love. She feels tremendous pride when exposing individuals to South Indian fare, a cuisine often underrepresented and unfamiliar to many.

Fishing and environmentalism have been a driving force in Fiona Lewis's life since she was a kid. Lewis spent her childhood in Australia fishing and watching her father studying fish species and devoting his energy to fish conservation. It only seemed natural that she'd follow in her father's footsteps and dive into the fish

Left: The District Fishwife's plentiful poke bowl. Photo courtesy of Jessica Burdge Photography. *Top center:* DC Dosa brimming with roasted vegetables and a variety of chutneys. *Above center:* DC Dosa delights stuffed with roasted vegetables and eggplant and sweet potatoes. Photos courtesy of Rochalle Stewart. *Right:* The District Fishwife's pan-fried house-made salmon burger. Photo courtesy of Jessica Burdge Photography.

industry. In 2014 Fiona, along with her partner Ben Friedman, opened District Fishwife, drawing upon 30 years of experience in restaurants, aquaculture, and environmental conservationism around the world.

Ten years later, their mission remains unchanged: providing their customers with fresh and healthy fish and shellfish that have been sustainably sourced and fished regionally. The couple's dedication to aquaculture and their passion for educating others is evident in the high quality of fish that they serve and their unyielding desire to ensure the health of our waterways. The couple also owns On Toast, a casual open-face sandwich stall, and Son of a Fish, a grab-and-go sushi spot.

Union Market
1309 5th St. NE, 301-347-3998
unionmarketdc.com

DC Dosa
National Landing Water Park:
1731 Crystal Dr., Arlington, VA
dcdosa.com

The District Fishwife
202-543-2592
thedistrictfishwife.com

Son of a Fish
sonofafishsushi.com

On Toast
ontoastdc.com

QUEEN'S ENGLISH

Long live the queen; relish the reign of Cantonese cooking

When husband-and-wife team Henji Cheung and Sarah Thompson were choosing a DC neighborhood, they had to ensure it passed the sniff test for one integral family member, their darling dog, Lucy Goose. The Manhattan transplants had visited Thompson's sister the prior year, throwing an elaborate dinner party for her sister's friends while testing out dishes and wine pairings. A month later, they had a new home in Columbia Heights, equipped with a yard for Lucy Goose, followed by a space for their dream eatery across the street. Today, the couple is proud to call the enclave home and share the cuisine of Chef Cheung's Hong Kong heritage with the community.

Cheung and Thompson met in the kitchens of Manhattan. They spent three years planning their restaurant, jotting down ideas with pen and paper. They wanted to add a modern twist to Cantonese cuisine, a regional cooking style they felt was underrepresented in the area.

Chef Cheung's menu exhibits a modern spin on Hong Kong dishes and is inspired by the flavors of his childhood and the years he spent as a chef. The white-hot wok is the foundation of Cantonese cooking. Dishes spotlight a harmonious blend of herbaceous

The Queen's English Natty Wine Club offers a monthly subscription of natural wines hand-selected by co-owner and wine aficionado Sara Thompson. Choose the number of bottles you'd like to receive each month: two bottles (staff favorites) four bottles (must-try wines of the season), or six bottles (staff favorites: collector's edition).

Left: Chef Henji Cheung at the helm of the kitchen. Photo courtesy of Hawkeye Johnson. *Center:* Crispy whole red snapper takes center stage. Photo courtesy of Albert Ting. *Right:* Owner and wine enthusiast Sarah Thompson pours one of her many carefully curated wines. Photo courtesy of Hawkeye Johnson.

ingredients and sizzling bold flavors like ginger and soy. Start off with plates like hamachi, brightened with soy, orange, and aromatic oils, and Mushroom Mushroom, a magnificent medley of royal trumpet mushrooms, pickled shimeji, and tofu. It would be criminal to miss out on the quartet of daikon fritters; the crispy, creamy, and custardy creation is the only dish that's remained on the menu since opening. As Thompson quips, there might be a revolt if they ever take the customer favorite off the menu. The crispy fried red snapper is another star among a galaxy of luminous offerings.

Wine paired with Chinese food? With Sarah Thompson leading the charge, the answer is an unequivocal YES. The wine aficionado seeks out off-the-beat natural wines that pair well with the dynamic flavors of her husband's dishes. Thompson leans toward skin-contact wines with a bit of tannin and higher acidity that can cut through the menu's robust flavors. Consider dipping your toes in the world of orange wine, or try the Red Misket, the Bulgarian blend favorite.

The restaurant's resplendent dining room is adorned with exemplary Chinese details mixed with polished contemporary furniture. Reserve a seat at the counter for a bird's-eye view of the chef-driven kitchen.

3410 11th St. NW, 202-618-1213
queensenglishdc.com

DOLCEZZA

A dream born in Argentina comes to life in DC

The sweet notion of Dolcezza was conceived in a gelateria over 5,000 miles south of DC. After meeting one another during a trip that began in the Brazilian Amazon and concluded in Sao Paulo, Violeta Edelman and Robb Duncan made their way to Edelman's homeland of Argentina. It was here at Freddo, a popular gelateria, that the lovestruck couple decided to create something incredible together.

Upon returning to the States, Edelman and Duncan began turning their dream into a reality. While the ambitious couple had no prior experience, they were determined to learn how to produce gelato with purpose and heart. They enlisted the help of a friend who devoted a month to training them. After that month of learning and diligently working to develop and master their recipes, they opened Dolcezza's doors in Georgetown. From the beginning, the couple has taken pride in sourcing fresh and seasonal ingredients like strawberries, quince, apples, and maple syrup from local farmers markets. They've built long-lasting relationships with farmers, including an Amish dairy farmer in Lancaster, Pennsylvaia, who has delivered milk twice a week for nearly 15 years! Edelman, Duncan, and their team produce small batches of handmade gelato each morning in their lab combining old-world practices with innovation and wonder. From melting chocolate to roasting spices and nuts, every single step is done with precision and care.

Choosing how to satisfy your sweet tooth may prove to be the real challenge here. Traditionalists can choose from classics like silky vanilla bean, decadent dark chocolate, and the pinnacle of sweet-and-salty goodness: salted caramel. More adventurous palates can choose from a sea of velvety flavors like sweet potato pecan praline, Thai coconut

Left: Melt-in-your-mouth goodness. *Center:* Grab a spoon and dig in. *Right:* Creamy dreamy pints of perfection. Photos courtesy of Dolcezza.

milk, and pistachio Siciliano. Dolcezza also blends up a handful of refreshingly luscious sorbettos like clementine and pomegranate.

Since its inception, Dolcezza has grown from 20 flavors to more than 200 and from one brick-and-mortar shop to multiple locations throughout the DMV area. Dolcezza is also sold in a number of grocery stores like Whole Foods and Yes! Organic Market.

As Duncan warmheartedly shares, "We didn't have any experience when we started. We just knew that we wanted to create something together, with our own hands, and that we and our family would be proud of." Just like the intoxicating tango dancers of Edelmen's home country, Dolcezza continues to dance across our taste buds, enrapturing us one creamy spoonful at a time.

Multiple locations
1704 Connecticut Ave. NW
dolcezzagelato.com

Dolcezza is the only local shop to open in a Smithsonian museum, operating a gelato trailer as well as a café in the lobby at the Hirshhorn Museum, offering a coffee service of drip coffee, espresso beverages, and hot teas.

THE GREEN ZONE

DC's only Middle Eastern bar

Why do people drink cocktails like White Russians when they could be drinking Middle Eastern cocktails instead? This was a question premier mixologist Chris Franke found himself asking during his four-year pop-up stint. His innovative concoctions quickly won acclaim and a loyal following. In 2018, Franke turned his pop-up concept into a full-blown cocktail bar, earning accolades and top spots on countless bar and cocktail lists ever since. Today, the Green Zone, DC's only Middle Eastern bar, continues to raise the bar by introducing guests to the vibrant and fragrant flavors of the region while infusing elements of pride, heritage, and ingenuity.

The Green Zone takes its name from the International Zone in Baghdad, symbolizing a safe space for individuals. Franke, who's half Iraqi and has family in Beirut, has not only created a watering hole centered around Middle Eastern culture, but has also cultivated a cause-focused space that serves as a community center and encourages others to be politically aware and question the status quo.

Franke realizes that when many think of cocktails, the Middle East may not be the first region to come to mind. He believes that the region has the best nonalcoholic beverages in the world, thus translating extraordinarily well into the cocktail realm. Some of Franke's favorite ingredients to experiment with include dried apricot syrup, orange blossom water, cardamom, and saffron. When asked to name his favorite spirit, Franke unequivocally answers, "Rum"; in fact, he hopes to open a rum bar soon. The bar's sweeping list of cocktails is categorized into three distinct sections. The Green Zone classics represent the libations launched during Franke's pop-up days, including A Few of My Favorite Things, a masterful

Left: The Double Apple—the Middle East's favorite smoking flavor. *Center:* Lebanese sampler of seasoned carrots, labneh, muhammara, falafel, hummus, shawarma, and more. *Right:* Fatteh—the popular Levantine dish of layers of crispy pita chips, spiced chickpeas, and a garlicky tahini yogurt sauce. Photos courtesy of the Green Zone.

blend of Ramallah Arak, Scotch, lemon, raw honey, and nostalgia; and Lebanese No. 1, coined as the Legend, a brilliant concoction of cognac, apricot, lemon, and "exotic stuff." Rotating seasonal and featured cocktails include the Desert Falcon, an amalgamation of Jamaican rum, pineapple, Campari, citrus, and Arabian flavors; and Jun Blossom, a spin on the classic martini.

From its music to its food, Middle Eastern culture permeates every crevice. The inventive cocktails pair magnificently with snacks like Lebanese falafel; Syrian muhammara scooped up on za'atar pita chips and Iraqi kubbat halab, crunchy rice shells filled with halal lamb and beef. More substantial fare like chicken shawarma and chicken pastilla round out a menu inspired by the foods Franke has enjoyed during his extensive travels.

2226 18th St. NW, 571-213-6588
thegreenzonedc.com

Visit the Green Zone's website for a list of their numerous events including Arabic and Middle Eastern music DJs every Friday night and international music DJs on Saturday nights.

WAGSHAL'S

Bite into something DELIcious at the "President's Deli"

Wagshal's has been feeding the region for nearly a century. From neighbors who have relied on the delicatessen for family dinners to renowned leaders like presidents stopping in for lunch, this legendary deli continues to be an integral part of DC's historical food scene.

In 1925, Sam Wagshal and his son, Ben, opened Wagshal's in Penn Quarter. Shortly thereafter, they expanded their business, eventually making their way to upper Northwest. They quickly became known for their corned beef, pâté, and 30-foot pickle barrel. The 1940s brought them a Supreme Court victory when they won against Bakery Sales Drivers Local Union 33, and the 1950s led them to catering Vice President Richard Nixon's birthday party at the National Press Club. Nixon wasn't the only president to adore Wagshal's; Presidents Harry S. Truman, Gerald Ford, and Dwight D. Eisenhower were also patrons, lending to the eatery's nickname, "The President's Deli."

In 1990, the Fuchs and Socha families purchased the delicatessen, and continue to operate it as a family-run business.

Today, Wagshal's is still recognized as one of Washington's premier delis and gourmet markets. They pride themselves on providing the highest quality of raw ingredients for sale in their market as well as their prepared foods. Their agglomerate of prime cuts and meats are processed as kosher from farms spanning from Pennsylvania to Virginia. Those looking for unique meats and game can choose from exotic offerings like antelope and elk. In addition to locally sourcing dairy, produce, and meat products, Wagshal's works closely

Left: Welcome to Wagshal's. *Center:* A bounty of bread awaits at Wagshal's. *Right:* Choose your cut of choice.

with local seafood purveyors. A tempting batch of breads, pastries, homemade Whoopie Pies and Twinkies, and more are baked fresh daily. Wagshal's also carries a wide array of boutique wines and spirits.

A sizeable selection of specialty, hot, and grilled sandwiches are served, including their award-winning smoked brisket, Italian and American cold cut sandwiches, veggie melts, and hoagies. Corned beef and pastrami sandwich favorites include their Reuben and the Super Double, which packs corned beef and pastrami into a triple-decker. Additional options like salads, soups, and build-your-own pizzas top off Wagshal's extensive menu.

A fun history fact worth noting: Sam Wagshal was the first person in line after Prohibition ended to obtain a DC liquor license. He showed up holding a blank check and asked the clerk, "How much do I make this out for?" Wagshal's proudly owns Washington, DC's, oldest liquor license.

Multiple locations
Main Location: 4855 Massachusetts Ave. NW, 202-363-5698
wagshals.com/delicatessen

LOVE, MAKOTO

A love letter to Japan

The DMV boasts a legion of chefs who masterfully compose the highest quality Japanese food. Few acts can compare to satiny slices of fish melting on your tongue or succulent cuts of Wagyu beef dancing across your taste buds. Among the elite is Chef Makoto Okuwa, the mastermind behind Love, Makoto, an impressive culinary collection of Japanese food and drink. Okuwa's love letter to Japan is a 20,000-square-foot sprawling food hub characterized by several distinct establishments. Grab your chopsticks and dive into some of the most exquisite Japanese fare the region has to offer.

Beloved BBQ, a Japanese steak house, boasts crimson-stained hallways evocative of a renowned Kyoto temple and smokeless grill tables designed for preparing Japanese A-5 Wagyu and American beef. Hiya Izakaya, a chic bar honoring Tokyo's

Top: Bluefin and Hamachi at Love Makoto's Dear Sushi. *Above:* O-toro at Love, Makoto's Dear Sushi. Photos courtesy of Mike Fuentes Photography.

bustling nightlife, is the perfect spot to sip on whiskey highballs and nosh on skewers and snacks. Dear Sushi highlights "old school" preparations alongside more cutting-edge "new school" takes. "Old school" melt-in-your-mouth hamachi, for example, is prepared with yuzu salt and shiso flower, while the "new school" version features smoked ponzu, chili paste, and cilantro. Love on the Run is the food hall's fast-casual concept, serving a wide array of Japanese fare including ramen, dumplings, and salads.

200 Massachusetts Ave. NW, Ste. 150, 202-992-7730
lovemakoto.com

NASIME

Unassuming brilliance in Old Town Alexandria

It's easy to walk by and miss one of the metropolitan area's best restaurants. Quietly situated amid the charming streets of Old Town Alexandria lies Nasime, an unassuming Japanese restaurant of just six counter seats and a handful of tables. Chef and owner Yuh Shimomura single-handedly prepares every aspect from scratch, employing his extensive training in Ginza, Tokyo, and over 15 years of culinary experience. You can't help but watch Shimomura as he adeptly maneuvers around his compact kitchen. The masterful chef has scrupulously designed Nasime's seven-course tasting menu to present an ambitious array of Japanese cuisine and create a superlative dining experience.

A parade of courses including Tsukuri (raw dishes), Yakimono (grilled dishes), and Agemono (fried dishes) highlights seasonal and traditional ingredients. While Nasime's menu changes daily, a typical dinner might start with edamame or chestnut surinagashi, a traditional Japanese soup, followed by seared Japanese Wagyu short rib and a ravishing rainbow explosion of otsukuri (sashimi plate).

Later courses might include fried Spanish octopus, charbroiled miso Chilean sea bass, and duck and matsutake mushroom udon noodle. A light and refreshing dessert of housemade ice creams top off the exquisite meal. From start to finish, Shimomura's level of precision and execution is truly exceptional.

1209 King St., Alexandria, VA, 703-548-1848
nasimerestaurant.com

Top: Otsukuri (sashimi). *Above:* House-made green tea ice cream will sweeten any special occasion.

SHARBAT

Tastes of Azerbaijan are as sweet as honey

Ilhama Safarova didn't intend to open a bakery when she immigrated to the US from Azerbaijan in 2018. The former nurse moved here so that her daughter, Shukrana, could attend college in DC. However, when she began sharing her baked confections with friends in the States, they encouraged her to transfer her talents from her home kitchen to a professional one. Thankfully for us Washingtonians, she followed their advice.

Safarova opened Sharbat bakery and café in the heart of Adams Morgan in the summer of 2021. Unique to the region, Sharbat introduces many to the foods of Azerbaijan, a cuisine enormously underrepresented in the United States. For the uninitiated, Azerbaijan is a former Soviet republic bordered by Russia, Georgia, Armenia, Turkey, and Iran. Sharbat boasts a luscious assortment of pastries evocative of Safarova's childhood and time spent in her homeland. Customers will find a gold mine inside of the bakery's cases, flushed with sweet and savory delights. Cakes take center stage at Sharbat, the most revered being the 32-layer honey cake embellished with a honeycomb imprint on top. Safarova's version of the Russian recipe that became popular during the Soviet rule of Azerbaijan until it gained independence in 1991 replaces whipped cream with sour cream that is distributed between exquisite layers of honeyed cake. Absheron cake, a traditional cake, is a favorite among the people of Baku, Azerbaijan's capital city. The walnut-speckled vanilla entremet is interspersed with silky layers of baked cream. The bakery's more familiar cake flavors include chocolate, carrot, raspberry, and apricot.

Another alluring pastry is Safarova's dazzling pakhlava, the Azerbaijani take on baklava. One batch of the 15-layered labor of

Top left: Savory meets sweet—the perfect combination. *Center left:* Flaky and fabulous pistachio pakhlava. *Bottom left:* An assortment of pastries to start your day off right. *Right:* Sharbat's bright and cheerful storefront in the heart of Adams Morgan.

love takes four hours to make. Shorgoghal is a traditional Azerbaijani pastry known for its round shape and is stuffed with a mixture of spices like anise, cumin, cinnamon, and turmeric. Unadulterated bliss awaits in every irresistible bite of Sharbat's baklava. The heavenly combination of honey-soaked layers of flaky phyllo pastry dotted with walnuts or pistachios will entrance you. Still hungry? Awaken your taste buds with badambura, a multilayered dessert filled with nuts, sugar, and aromatic spices.

2473 18th St. NW, 202-843-5252

BEN'S CHILI BOWL

A testament to African American history, culture, and character

On August 22, 1958, Ben and Virginia Ali turned a dream into a renowned DC institution when they opened Ben's Chili Bowl on U Street. It's here where their legacy began and their place in DC history and culture was cemented. The building the couple chose was the former site of DC's first silent movie house, the Minnehaha, established in 1911. Once dubbed as "Black Broadway," U Street was a thriving enclave of African American culture. Many jazz legends, including Duke Ellington, Nat King Cole, and Miles Davis, would stop by Ben's after performing at U Street clubs. Ben's commitment to the community was further evident during the 1968 race riots following the assassination of Dr. Martin Luther King Jr. Immediately following that tragic moment in Memphis, the streets of our nation's capital endured eight straight days of violent rioting and raging fires, resulting in the deaths of at least ten people. Ben's found itself at the center of events when they became the only restaurant allowed to stay open past the citywide curfew. The spot quickly became a refuge and safe space for many, including activists, local police officers, and firemen.

Now, over 60 years later, Ben's has expanded beyond their flagship U Street location with multiple locations on H Street, Nationals Stadium, Reagan National Airport, and the DC Convention Center. Every August 22, Ben's celebrates their birthday, as well as African American history, culture, and the resilience of DC and the Greater U Street Historic District.

The DC institution has mastered comfort food. Perhaps Ben's biggest draw is its half-smoke, widely regarded as DC's original and

Left: Young Virginia Ali at the U Street location. *Center:* Ben's Chili Bowl lights up U Street. *Right:* Ben and Virginia on their wedding day in 1958. Photos courtesy of Ben's Chili Bowl.

most famous. Craving a cup or bowl of chili? As their name suggests, there's no shortage of their popular homemade chili; choose from con carne, turkey, or veggie. Can't decide? Here you can have the best of both worlds and top your favorite half-smokes, burgers, and hot dogs with mild or spicy chili. Their extensive list of vegetarian options, including veggie burgers and dogs, has won awards from PETA. No need to look any further when that sugar craving hits: hand-spun milkshakes and Virginia's favorite banana pudding will do the trick.

As one of DC's most venerable landmarks, Ben's has welcomed a bevy of politicians and celebrities throughout the years, including Presidents Barack Obama and George Bush, musicians Bono and Mary J. Blige, and comedians Dave Chapelle and Chris Rock.

Multiple locations
The Original Location: 1213 U St. NW, 202-667-0909
benschilibowl.com

For those looking for a taste of Ben's at home, Ben's offers catering options including buffet-style meals, platters, and individually packed meals. They also ship samplers of their renowned specialties nationwide.

L'AUBERGE CHEZ FRANÇOIS

The way it's supposed to be

The sprawling grounds that have become synonymous with L'Auberge Chez François look remarkably different from what they were in its early days. Trailblazer François Haeringer opened the original brasserie in 1954 in downtown DC. In 1975, the hotel that housed it was sold, leaving Haeringer in search of another location. He embraced the opportunity to explore Virginia's countryside in hopes of fulfilling a lifelong dream: opening an auberge (French for country inn) akin to those in his Alsatian hometown of Obernai. Driving through the rolling hills of Great Falls, François became enamored by an expansive stretch of land. He purchased the six-acre lot and opened his French country-style inn in 1976. Today, his son Chef Jacques laughs as he recalls the inn's disastrous opening night. Not wanting to turn away loyal patrons, the restaurant was overbooked, causing them to run out of food. As if on cue, a severe storm left them without power, forcing hungry patrons to be sent home without dinner. The rest, as Jacques quips, is history.

Jacques was 11 years old when he began working at the family restaurant. He later traveled to France to attend culinary school followed by stints at high-end establishments. Today, Jacques and his brother Paul continue to follow in their late father's footsteps, serving classic and contemporary French cuisine. While Jacques relishes opportunities to be playful when reinterpreting French classics, he's also serious about preserving the restaurant's core and his father's culinary vision. Many of their longtime patrons have come to depend on familiar mainstays, so much that when the restaurant was damaged by a fire in 2000, regulars repeatedly sought out reassurance that nothing would change, including its menu. As Jacques affectionately notes, they are the keeper of memories, as

Top left: Le Homurd du Maine—Maine lobster, jumbo lump crabmeat, citrus, and sauternes sauce. *Above left:* Grande tente garden terrace. *Top right:* L'Auberge Chez François's front entrance. *Above right:* Chef Jacques by the garden. Photos courtesy of James Diedrich.

generations have chosen L'Auberge to celebrate their life milestones. Patrons "want what they want," and Chef and his team are more than happy to oblige. As Papa François used to say, "It's the way it's supposed to be."

One of Jacques's greatest sources of joy is his two large gardens. He devotes countless hours tending to his lettuce, peppers, cabbage, and broccoli. He especially enjoys visiting dinner tables with an armful of vegetables from the season's harvest. Moreover, L'Auberge is acutely aware of its carbon footprint, adopting recycling and composting practices as well as working with organic farms and purveyors. For a more casual affair, head to the Brasserie and Bar Rouge, located in the back lower level of the inn.

332 Springvale Rd., Great Falls, VA, 703-759-3800
laubergechezfrancois.com

CHAIA

Making the world a better place, one taco at a time

It all started at a book club. With hopes of improving her cooking and entertaining skills, Bettina Stern formed a cookbook club, where a mutual friend introduced her to Suzanne Simon. The two women hit it off, both sharing an interest for food, often cooking scratch-made meals for their families. And so, a budding partnership began, built upon a joint passion for fresh and tasty ingredients along with a healthy obsession with tacos.

The duo dove headfirst into the food world. They began teaching cooking classes, and in 2007 they launched a food blog where they wrote about cooking and DC's burgeoning food scene. Blogs were not as common as they are today, and their blog soon captured the interests and appetites of many. The women's take on food quickly garnered attention within the industry, and in 2012 Stern and Simon were invited to participate in a start up kitchen competition. Shortly afterward, they opened a "farm to taco" stand at the White House Farmers Market. Hungry lunch-goers ranging from White House chefs to government employees began swarming around their stand, savoring the flavorful combinations of locally sourced vegetables enveloped by homemade corn tortillas and topped with fresh salsas. They sold out day after day, working feverishly to keep up with the demand. Soon they landed a highly coveted spot at DC's esteemed Dupont Market and were featured in the *Washington Post*. It was clear they had cemented their space in DC's vibrant food scene.

Farmers' markets, however, were just the beginning for the twosome. Stern and Simon devised a business plan, and on November 19, 2015, the first Chaia brick-and-mortar opened in Georgetown.

Left: Moroccan carrot taco with goat cheese, chipotle yogurt sauce, and mint. *Center:* Brussels sprout quesadilla. *Right:* Sweet potato nachos. Photos courtesy of Steve Vilnit.

Years later they've expanded across the DMV, adding additional locations in Chinatown and Bethesda, Maryland. While Chaia has grown significantly throughout the years, Stern and Simon have never strayed from their mission: getting people to eat more fresh vegetables, one flavorful taco at a time. They've stuck to what they know best, offering six taco creations at a time that highlight locally sourced vegetables at the peak of harvest and growing season. Vegetables continue to be the stars of the show, their unique and delicate flavors enhanced through a variety of cooking methods like roasting, braising, and sautéing. Handmade tortillas are carefully created with organic, gluten-free masa and griddled to order. House-made salsas and creamy cheeses add the finishing touches to a handheld creation that's nothing short of perfection.

Multiple locations
Original location: 3207 Grace St. NW, 202-333-5222
chaiatacos.com

Large taco trays are available to order for group gatherings and celebrations. Chaia can accommodate dietary restrictions and allergies when requests are made in advance.

HELLBENDER BREWING COMPANY

A better way to brew beer

When German brewmaster Christian Heurich founded DC's original brewery in 1872, now home to the world-renowned John F. Kennedy Center, he never could have imagined that his innovative beer production would eventually pave the way for the dozens of breweries that have enhanced DC's beverage scene. Brewing techniques have evolved significantly over the years, with many breweries becoming more aware of their environmental footprint. At the forefront is Hellbender Brewing Company, a brewery committed to sustainable brewing processes and proving that there's a "better way to brew beer."

Beer aficionado and former neuroscience researcher Ben Evans has been brewing beer for years, dating back to his college days when he purchased an at-home brewing kit to make craft beer with his family. After years of research, apprenticing on weekends while pursuing his graduate degree at the University of Maryland, and working years to devise a thorough business plan, Evans fulfilled his longtime dream and opened Hellbender Brewing Company in November 2014.

Ben's childhood obsession with amphibians and passion for sustainability led to the naming of Hellbender, a two-foot amphibian that is endangered in the wild. Staying true to his commitment to the environment, Evans has gone to great lengths to ensure that Hellbender Brewing Company is environmentally conscious driven. Hellbender was the first brewery on the East Coast to invest in a mash filter system and remains one of the only breweries to use this system.

The mash filter is an environmental game changer, allowing Hellbender to brew 25 percent more efficiently while using 30 percent less water and 18 percent less grain than traditional breweries. Grains are grinded to a fine powder through a hammer mill allowing for more starches to be exposed, an integral part of the malting and brewing processes. While a typical brewery mash extracts between 75 and 80 percent of starches, Hellbender's system extracts a whopping 98 percent.

Some of Hellbender's most popular beers include their Bare Bones Kolsch and Southern Torrent saison; the OG beers have been fixtures here since the beginning. Hellbender leans heavily towards German-style lagers and hazy IPAs with Kellerbier, Festbier, and Turtle Frog leading the charge while also departing from their usual offerings with beers like Cherry on Top, a cherry kettle sour.

A devout believer in the value of local partnerships, Evans prides himself on partnering with local farmers, malting companies, and food trucks. Featured food trucks change regularly, ranging from African fare to tacos and brick-oven pizza.

5788 2nd St. NE, 202-827-8768
hellbenderbeer.com

ALBI | YELLOW

Levantine fare from the heart and hearth

Navy Yard superstar Albi has been wowing diners since chef and owner Michael Rafidi opened its doors to instantaneous acclaim. Meaning "the heart" in Arabic, Albi's cuisine pays homage to Rafidi's Levantine ancestry. Its convivial dining room is centered on its roaring hearth, creating a swoon-worthy gastronomic expedition that transports diners to the very heart of a bustling medina one might stumble upon in the Middle East.

Raised in Maryland, Chef Rafidi skillfully blends his mid-Atlantic upbringing with his Levantine roots to create masterpieces derived from his Palestinian background along with his research trips through Lebanon. Albi's diverse hummus selection is proof that not all hummus is created equal. Two knockouts, the Maryland crab and coal-fired mushroom, are served alongside their perfectly charred pita. Satisfy your senses with a wondrous tour of mezze that include the season's bountiful produce and ingredients like sumac carrots and embered asparagus. Feast on mashawi, Arab food staples consisting of barbecued meat, chicken, and fish, along with shawarma-style meats.

Their comprehensive wine menu reads more like a collection of enlightening essays depicting histories, tidbits, and even a love letter to Chateau Musar, a family-run winery in Lebanon that's stood the test of time. The lengthy list highlights varieties from lesser-known regions like Lebanon, Georgia, and Palestine. Unique and cleverly categorized wines like "The Godfather" reds, "Donnie Darko" reds, and #Unicornwines lend to an imaginative and whimsical wine experience.

Guests looking for an even more elevated evening should consider booking the Hearth Table for Chef Rafidi's Sofra, a semi-

Left: Albi chef and owner Michael Rafidi. *Top center:* Sweet and savory pastries at YELLOW. *Above center:* Albi's wood-fired pizza surrounded by a sumptuous spread of mezze. *Right:* Feast on Albi's melt-in-your-mouth kebobs. Photos courtesy of Rey Lopez.

improvisational tasting menu and bird's-eye view of their stunning open kitchen. Throughout an impressive 2.5-hour dining experience, chefs prepare a spontaneous menu showcasing peak season ingredients. Two optional wine pairings are also available.

Chef Rafidi's YELLOW is a more casual café affair. Their Levantine menu spotlights sweet and savory pastries, wood-fired pita sandwiches, and mezze. In need of a jolt? YELLOW's carefully crafted coffee menu is what coffee dreams are made of. Be assured; this is not your run-of-the-mill coffee shop.

A visit to Albi and YELLOW promises a multifaceted experience melding ancient tradition and exemplary cooking.

Albi
1346 4th St. SE, 202-921-9592
albidc.com

YELLOW
Multiple locations
YELLOW HQ @ Union Market
1309 5th St. NE
yellowthecafe.com

149

BEAU THAI

Three's company in delightfully approachable Thai cuisine

Some of Aschara Vigsittaboot's most sentimental childhood memories involve visiting the local markets near her southern Thailand home. She frequented the stalls of her friends' parents to purchase meat and produce. As the eldest daughter of five children, Vigsittaboot was often responsible for cooking for her family. When she would return from the market, she would ask her mother how to prepare different dishes. These market trips, coupled with cooking alongside her mother, fueled Vigsittaboot's ardor for cooking and desire to share the food of her homeland with others.

When Vigsittaboot came to the US to join her brother, she only intended to stay for six months. She worked as a server at Rice and soon months turned into years. Aschara's enthusiasm for cooking was as fervent as when she was a little girl, and she found herself dreaming of opening a restaurant of her own. She recalls watching the chefs, knowing that she could cook just as well as they could.

Vigsittaboot met present-day business partners and husbands Ralph Brabham and Drew Porterfield at Rice and sometimes cooked for them on the weekends. A budding friendship emerged as the three bonded over shared meals. Vigsittaboot enlisted their help and

Since its inception, Beau Thai has earned countless accolades and resounding praise from their devoted following. They are also committed to giving back to the surrounding communities, serving as loyal contributors to numerous local organizations like Ayuda, Horton's Kids, Bread for the City, and La Clinica Del Pueblo.

Left: Full-on feast at Beau Thai. *Right:* Cheers from founder Aschara Vigsittaboot. Photos courtesy of Reema Desai.

asked them to partner with her in opening a small Thai eatery. It was only a matter of time until the trio would expand upon their vision and introduce Vigsittaboot's traditional Thai cooking to multiple communities around the District.

In 2010, Vigsittaboot, Brabham, and Porterfield opened their first Beau Thai location followed by a second outpost in 2013. Vigsittaboot designed a simple Thai menu, reflective of one you'd come across while traveling through Thailand. While she's made some changes over the years (like cutting out certain dishes when she couldn't find fresh seafood like she used to find back home), most dishes have withstood the test of time. She lists lemongrass, Thai chilies, shrimp paste, garlic, and curry paste, which Beau Thai makes from scratch, as some of her favorite ingredients to cook with. While menu items like drunken noodles and pad Thai are favorites among customers, the Udom's curry carries a special significance for Vigsittaboot. The soothing, velvety spiced dish is lovingly named after Vigsittaboot's mother. It is prepared similarly to the panang curry Vigsittaboot ate as a child, reminiscent of her earlier years in Thailand and the woman who had a profound influence on Vigsittaboot as a chef and an individual.

1550 7th St. NW, 202-536-5636
3162 Mount Pleasant St. NW, 202-450-5317
beauthaidc.com

151

TIMBER PIZZA CO. | CALL YOUR MOTHER DELI

From the back of a Chevy truck to building a culinary empire

The moment I meet Andrew Dana at a Takoma Park coffee shop, he hands me a jar of peanut butter. The all-natural spread is just the latest culinary venture of his and wife/partner Dani Moreira. His excitement around their newest adventure is palpable, and within minutes it's abundantly clear that this dynamic duo flourishes whenever they create something together.

Growing up in Mount Pleasant, Andrew's father practiced law, but his dream was to open a deli. Andrew attended business school and worked at an educational software start-up, but like his father, he had dreams of opening an eatery, something that would unmistakably be his and that he could create with his hands. He bought a mobile wood-fired pizza oven and began testing pizza recipes in his parents' bathtub and in alleyways; no place was off limits. By 2014, Andrew had launched Timber Pizza Co., a mobile pizzeria, where he fired up pies from a baby-blue 1967 Chevy truck at local farmers markets and kids' birthday parties. It was at a farmers market during a lighthearted battle over a carton of eggs that Andrew met his wife and partner, Dani. After four months of begging Dani to be Timber's head chef, she finally agreed, and the powerhouse partnership officially commenced.

> Both Timber Pizza and Call Your Mother have been named among *Bon Appétit's* 50 Best New Restaurants lists, Timber Pizza in 2017 and Call Your Mother in 2019.

Left: A tall order at Timber Pizza. *Right:* Pretty in pink at Call Your Mother. Photos courtesy of Tim Casey.

In 2016 the brick-and-mortar Timber Pizza Co. opened in Petworth. The Neapolitan-ish pizza joint was an instant hit, soon distinguished by the winding lines forming outside its doors. Standouts include the Green Monster, a pesto-based vegetarian staple since its early farmers market days; the Bentley; and their empanadas, a nod to Dani's Argentinian roots.

Two years later, Call Your Mother Deli, Andrew's father's longtime dream and tribute to his Jewish family and faith, opened. Some of Andrew's fondest memories include visiting his grandparents in Boca Raton with food being at the core of those trips. Fittingly, bagels, schmearz, fixin's, and deli classics lead the Jew-ish inspired lineup.

Years later, one key lesson resonates with Andrew: it's impossible to compete with memories associated with someone's grandmother's matzah ball soup or other foods steeped in family tradition, even if your recipe is amazing. Instead, focus on your creation and how you can put your own spin on it. With so much success, some may ask, what else could Andrew and Dani possibly accomplish? Peanut butter made from Argentinian peanuts, naturally.

Timber Pizza Co.
809 Upshur St. NW, 202-853-9746
timberpizza.com

Call Your Mother Deli
Multiple locations
The Original Location: 3301 Georgia
Ave. NW, 202-450-5307
callyourmotherdeli.com

XIQUET

Exquisite Valencian fare with a taste of home

This Michelin-starred, showstopping restaurant transports diners to the Spanish coastal city of Valencia, where Chef Danny Lledó draws upon his Valencian and Portuguese heritages. A Takoma Park native who has also spent years living in the small Valencian town of Dénia, Chef Lledó grew up learning from his chef father and his family full of farmers and fishermen. Xiquet (pronounced chee-KETT), is a Catalan colloquialism meaning "local kid/boy," reflecting the term of endearment Danny's father used for him. Lledó's blockbuster boasts an ambitious tasting menu of over 20 innovative courses expertly cooked in a wood-fired kitchen. The converted three-story Georgetown home provides an intimate setting while offering a sophisticated dining experience. Lledó and his team create a spellbinding experience in which guests feel as if they have been invited into Lledó's home, encouraging them to linger for a while and bask in its splendor and hospitality.

The Chef's Menu, an elaborate ensemble of Valencian-inspired plates, changes seasonally according to the availability of key ingredients. While some dishes come and go or are altered depending on ingredient availability, there's one dish that is a constant fixture. As an ode to the birth city of paella, a Valencian rice dish prepared over a wood fire in a paella pan always graces Xiquet's menu. One recent rice dish, arrós a banda, highlights red prawn of Dénia, tuna belly, cuttlefish, and Petrossian ossetra caviar, cooked according to the Alicante paella method.

Xiquet's gastronomic affair commences at the first floor's Chef's Counter, where diners are treated to mouthwatering canapés, aperitivos, and a warm welcome by Lledó. Next, guests are escorted

upstairs to the minimalist six-table dining room for the bulk of the night. Heading to your table, it's nearly impossible not to marvel at Chef's dramatic wood-fired kitchen encased in glass. An evening at Xiquet is one to be savored, recounted, and remembered. Relish lavish courses like grilled octopus accompanied by grapes, orange pearls, and caviar, and brioche with hokkaido uni and plankton butter. Larger plates like Wellington Ibéric (pork tenderloin and Ibérico ham delicately enveloped in puff pastry and drizzled with ibéric jus) and Colomi (a dry-aged squab breast accentuated with foie mousse, morels, figs, and squab sauce) are nothing short of extraordinary.

The majestic soiree winds down in their sleek mezzanine lounge with a grand after-dinner drinks-and-dessert finale. Sweet enticements have included paté de fruits, semifreddo, turnovers, and bonbons.

2404 Wisconsin Ave. NW, 202-913-4671
xiquetdl.com

Xiquet's prix-fixe menu is set at a fixed cost with the option of adding enhancements like wine pairings at an additional cost. Chef Lledó is also a sommelier and works closely with his team in creating the pairings. Many of Xiquet's rarer wines are from Lledó's personal collection and allocations.

ROAMING ROOSTER

Fried chicken you can feel good about

In today's era of social media, one should never underestimate the power of a tweet, especially once it's gone viral. Just ask brothers Michael and Biniyam Habtemariam and sister-in-law/wife Hareg Mesfin, founders of Roaming Rooster. Amid the contentious fried chicken war between heavy hitters Popeyes and KFC in 2019, a local woman tweeted, "While Popeyes is cool and all if you live in the DMV area you should check out Roaming Rooster in DC. It's Black owned, and the founder Mike is Ethiopian born. He grew the family business from a food truck and has always been kind." The tweet spawned a slew of retweets and additional tweets singing its praises. The following morning, Mike arrived at his northeast location greeted by a line of more than 100 customers eager to see what all the fuss was about. In a blink of a tweet, the trajectory of Roaming Rooster had been forever changed.

Food has always been at the core of the Habtemariam family. Their father, an Ethiopian Air Force pilot, lost his left hand in a plane crash, causing much of the cooking responsibilities to fall on the two brothers. They learned to cook a wide range of cuisines including Ethiopian, vegetarian, Indian, and American. They grew up working in restaurants and eventually drew upon their experience to launch a falafel food truck

Need more fried chicken in your life? Michelin-studded Chef Elias Taddesse melds his Ethiopian roots and Minneapolis upbringing in his Ethiopian-style fried chicken at highly acclaimed Doro Soul Food while Texas-born, Louisiana-raised lauded Chef Kevin Tien brings his culinary brilliance to Hot Lola's, a Nashville-meets-Sichuan fried-chicken joint.

Top: Chicken piled high with a side of fries. *Bottom:* The Club. Photos courtesy of Laura Nockett.

cleverly dubbed DC Ballers. As they traveled around, they noticed a glaring void of fried chicken options. The brothers spent over two years experimenting with recipes, only using free-range, grain-fed, and antibiotic halal chicken. In 2015, Roaming Rooster's wheels were set into motion, entering full speed into DC's food truck scene. They received tremendous acclaim, selling out daily before lunch service ended.

By 2018 it was clear that Roaming Rooster needed a bigger kitchen. Their first location started as a depot before eventually converting into its first brick-and-mortar. Five years later, Roaming Kitchen has expanded their team and presence with 11 (and counting!) locations spanning across the region. The Habtemariam family is steadfast in serving fried chicken that individuals can feel good about. Their chickens are raised in a humane and natural manner, never given antibiotics or chemicals of any kind. They work exclusively with free-range chicken farms where birds have an abundance of sunshine, ample roaming space, and natural vegetation. In addition to their revered fried chicken sandwiches, Roaming Rooster's offerings include wings, tenders, and milkshakes.

Multiple locations
3176 Bladensburg Rd. NE
www.roamingroosterdc.com

WESTERN MARKET & NIM ALI SHUKOS

Traditional Guatemalan fare shines brightly at Foggy Bottom's newest food hub

While the recently opened Western Market may look shiny and new, its origins can be traced to 1802. Along with Eastern and Central Markets, Western Market was part of the city's three original marketplaces, devised by urban planner Pierre L'Enfant. Of these three historic markets, the only one left standing is Capitol Hill's Eastern Market. The city sold Western Market in 1965 and shortly thereafter it was demolished. Foggy Bottom's newest culinary hub, which stands across from the original market, is evocative of the marketplace's early days. Today Western Market serves as a convivial gathering place for college students and food and drink enthusiasts alike.

One of the market's premier merchants is Nim Ali Shukos, a Guatemalan street food operation conceived by married couple Karla Alonzo and Rosario Guzman. Bright vivid colors along with throngs of customers crowding the stall make the market favorite easy to spot. Nim Ali Shukos began as a pop-up at Jake's Tavern in Shaw in 2020 and quickly evolved into a culinary force that's amassed a devoted following. Noticing a lack of Guatemalan cuisine in the Washington, DC, region, the couple brought traditional fare from Alonzo's Guatemalan homeland along with other dishes from throughout Mexico and Central America. "Nim Ali" denotes a strong Mayan queen, an honorable nickname often given to female family leaders in Alonzo's hometown of San Lorenzo.

Patrons flock here for Nim Ali's kaleidoscope-colored shukos, traditional Guatemalan hot dogs. The original is a beast of a feast:

Center: Welcome to Western Market. *Top right:* All smiles at Nim Ali Shukos. *Bottom right:* Mix and match—there's something for everyone at Western Market. Photos courtesy of Western Market.

a foot-long beef hot dog stuffed inside a toasted bun topped with guacamole, escabeche slaw, and drizzles of ketchup, mustard, mayonnaise, and picamas. Other shukos feature grilled or fried chicken, asada (steak), chorizo, bacon, adobada (marinated pork), and a vegan protein. Guzman's birthplace of Puebla, Mexico, is reflected in the menu's antojitos, Mexican street food, which literally translates to "little cravings." Choose from a wide array of these tasty snacks including elote loco, tamalitos, tostadas, empanadas, and enchiladas. Desayunos, or breakfast foods, include pan con huevos y jamón (egg-and-ham breakfast sandwich) and breaks burritos. Sweet treats include churros, fried plantains, and rellenitos, a traditional Guatemalan dessert made with mashed plantains filled with sweet black beans.

Follow Nim Ali Shukos on social media to find out where their popular food truck will be parked around the DMV area. Special pop-up events and culinary collaborations are also featured.

Western Market
2000 Pennsylvania Ave. NW, #3500
westernmarketdc.com

Nim Ali Shukos
Food Truck:
clover.com/online-ordering/
nim-ali--washington

> **Visit Western Market's website and Instagram page to learn more about events like Trivia Night and special pop-up shops.**

STABLE

From the Swiss Alps to the H Street Corridor

While David Fritsche and Silvan Kraemer initially believed their first encounter occurred while working in Dubai's hospitality industry, their paths had unknowingly crossed decades before in Switzerland when David Fritsche was 13 years old. Now in their seventh year as co-owners of the only full-service Swiss restaurant on the East Coast outside of Manhattan, neither could have ever imagined that chance interaction so many years ago would have led them along this incredible journey.

Chef Fritsche's cooking path began in his grandmother's hotel in the Swiss Alps. He helped by restocking the buffet and preparing simple dishes and fell in love with the energy of the restaurant industry. One cooking lesson at age 12 was all Manager Kraemer needed to know that he wanted to pursue a culinary career. Following their culinary apprenticeships back home in Switzerland, both men took their talents abroad, working in some of the world's most prestigious establishments in Dubai, Cork, and Manhattan before settling in DC. After years of working for others, they decided to quit their jobs and open a restaurant together.

Stable wasn't initially a Swiss-focused concept, but after noticing a void in the space, Fritsche and Kraemer decided to test the waters

Stable has everything you need for the perfect outdoor picnic. Choose from three brilliant baskets: Rosé in the Park, Beers and Pretzels, or Brunch on a Bench. All baskets include a blanket, disposable plates, silverware, and cups as well as the wicker basket itself. Visit their website for more information and prices.

and host a pop-up. The overwhelmingly positive response convinced them to take the plunge and introduce the city to Swiss cuisine. Whether you're new to Swiss food or have been enjoying it for years, you're guaranteed to fall in love with this cozy neighborhood gem. Try favorites like vol-au-vent, a comforting puff pastry served with chicken dumplings and vegetables, and veal Zurich style. Seasonal dishes like spring risotto and salad shine a luminous light on vegetables like asparagus and garden peas, while meat marvels like herb-crusted pork loin, duck rillette, and Italian speck will satiate even the most discerning palates. Don't miss Stable's weekend brunch, where you can feast on darlings like bratwurst, schnitzel, potato pancakes, and house-made bakery items like Berliners, breads, and buttery croissants.

For a truly unique and authentic experience, indulge in Stable's Traditional Swiss Cheese Fondue or book their Unlimited Raclette Experience, Switzerland's iconic belly-warming cheese dish prepared tableside. Raclette is both the name of the Swiss cheese and the grill it's prepared on. Prepared in its homeland's traditional style, the creamy, salty, slightly sweet, and pungent Swiss superstar is served with potatoes, pickles, onion salad, green salad, and house-made Wurzel bread.

1324 H St. NE, 202-733-4604
stabledc.com

MASSERIA

Rustically refined Italian cooking

Growing up in Maryland, Nicholas Stefanelli was often surrounded by two things: family and food. His affinity for cooking was nurtured in a household where food was at the heart of daily life. Stefanelli's Italian and Greek grandparents both loved to cook. Unbeknownst to them, they helped shape their grandson's career path.

While traveling throughout Italy in the late 1990s, Stefanelli was captivated by the country's rustic yet refined cuisine. He was baffled by the stark difference between the food he had tasted abroad and the food he was accustomed to in the States. Stefanelli shares that American cuisine in the '90s was nothing like the imaginative fare it is today, and it couldn't hold a candle to that of Italy and other neighboring nations. He had found his calling during this portentous trip and set out on a course that would dramatically change American cuisine for the better.

Stefanelli enrolled in L'Academie de Cuisine and proceeded to work at a multitude of distinguished Italian restaurants throughout the region, including working under the tutelage of Roberto Donna at Galileo and Fabio Trabocchi at Maestro. In 2009 Stefanelli was recruited by restaurateur Ashok Bajaj to develop the menu and lead the kitchen at the late Bibiana.

In 2015, the acclaimed chef opened Masseria, an Italian-inspired oasis within NoMa's Union Market district. While NoMa is now regarded as one of DC's most sought-after neighborhoods, it's important to note that Masseria is largely responsible for putting the neighborhood on DC's dining map, serving as the leading force behind its rapid growth and popularity. Italian for *farmhouse*, Masseria pays homage to the fine Italian cooking of Stefanelli's childhood

Left: Seppia (cuttlefish). *Center:* Grab a seat and stay a while inside Masseria's dining room. Photos courtesy of Scott Suchman. *Right:* Masseria chef and owner Nicholas Stefanelli. Photo courtesy of Masseria.

and the southeastern Italian region of Puglia, where his family has its roots. When curating menus, he allows the flow of seasons and availability of ingredients to dictate dishes, comparing the change of seasons to new sets of paints he and his team look forward to playing with. While the chef doesn't like to play favorites when it comes to the ingredients he enjoys working with, there's one meal he simply can't go without: pasta, the heralded dish of his ancestors.

Every detail of Stefanelli's modern coastal Italian cuisine is meticulously planned and plated from the highest-quality ingredients. Masseria invites guests to "Vestiti per soddisfare gli altri, ma mangia per soddisfare te stesso"—Dress to satisfy others but eat to satisfy yourself.

1340 4th St. NE, 202-608-1330
masseria-dc.com

Diners can choose from two dining experiences: a special eight-course Chef's Tasting Menu at the Chef's Table and Chef's Counter and a six-course La Cucina Menu at the bar, sala, and pergola. In addition to earning one Michelin Star, Masseria has been recognized by *50 Top Italy* at number 12 among the Best Italian Restaurants in the World outside of Italy.

THE BLOCK FOODHALL

The DMV's first Asian food hall

Gastronomads looking for a tasting tour of the globe's largest continent need look no farther than the DMV area. The region's first Asian food hall is a foodie mecca of Asia-centric fare celebrating its rich and vibrant cuisines.

Don't let the Block's Virginia location's surrounding strip mall and nearby Kmart fool you. Inside Annandale's lively food hall lie 5,000 square feet bursting with flavorful food, dessert, and drinks. Six unique concepts make up the aptly named space designed to embody the convivial atmosphere of a neighborhood block party. Balo Kitchen prides itself on serving Asian classics with a modern twist. Dan-dan noodles, bahn-mi, and grilled street corn are just a few standouts on Balo's extensive menu. Meaning "backpack" in Vietnamese, the slang term "Balo" is a nod to the throngs of Western backpackers traveling throughout the southeast Asian nation. At the Chinese-Mongolian inspired Bold Dumpling, a variety of dumplings stuffed with savory fillings like pork and deep-fried kimchi serve as the marquee dishes. SnoCream Company, a vibrant Taiwanese shaved ice and bubble tea concept, was founded by Arturo Mei. After leaving his career in finance, Mei took time to travel throughout Asia; it was there that the idea of SnoCream was conceived. This Taiwanese specialty involves blocks of ice cream rapidly shaved into paper-thin snow ribbons. The result? A light and fluffy frozen dessert. From humble beginnings working out of a Sno Bus, SnoCream eventually expanded to a storefront stall as its popularity grew. Try taro or black sesame sno drizzled with caramel sauce topped by one of their 30 toppings like mochi and Frosted Flakes.

About 20 miles north via I-495 stands the Block's Maryland location in Bethesda's bustling Pike & Rose center. For an antioxidant boost

164

Left: The Block at Pike & Rose. *Right:* Sushi Oma. Photos courtesy of Thomas Piantone.

and caffeine and sugar fixes, head to Kyoto Matcha, an international chain specializing in matcha desserts and drinks. Cool down with some matcha soft serve, matcha lemonade, or a matcha latte float. Those looking to indulge can choose from a mouthwatering array of matcha-infused cakes like matcha red bean towel cake, matcha cheese mousse cake, and matcha crepe layer cake. Head to Sushi Oma's for sushi and raw oysters. Hand rolls range from the traditional like California and spicy tuna to more eclectic finds like spam musubi and sweet potato tempura. A selection of nigiri and sashimi along with OmaFish Bowls and Boxes highlighting heaps of rice topped with an assortment of raw fish and avocado and cucumber help round out their extensive menu. Grab a seat at their oyster bar to slurp back some sweet and briny oysters from the Chesapeake Bay. Make your way to Kitch Hibachi & Noodle Bar for wonton and dumpling soups, chicken, beef, shrimp, or tofu teriyaki, and rice dishes starring the likes of Chinese barbecue pork and General Tso's Tofu.

4221 John Marr Dr., Annandale, VA
703-942-5076

967 Rose Ave., North Bethesda, MD
301-770-8900

theblockfoodhall.com

AGORA

Turkish delight

Turkish food is one of the world's most varied and colorful cuisines. Like the nation's diverse cultural composition, the food of Turkey encompasses flavors and influences derived from many of its neighboring regions. Its culinary landscape has evolved over centuries, shaped by the influences of the Byzantine and Ottoman Empires, and inspired by the mosaic of cultures and flavors that continue to contribute to the vibrant cuisine we enjoy today.

Agora (the name referring to an open-air gathering place) is one of the region's most acclaimed Turkish restaurants. Manager Hakan Alagoz shares that when he sought out a Turkish establishment upon his arrival from Turkey, choosing where he wanted to work was simple; Agora was the best Turkish restaurant he had eaten at in the area. The first time Hakan tasted Agora's Adana kebap, a kebab of minced lamb and New York strip steak served with grilled tomato and sumac onions, he was transported back home, captivated by the taste. He drew upon his experience in the restaurant industry and soon became an integral member of the Agora team. Hakan describes Turkey as the bridge between a swath of countries throughout Europe, Asia, and the Middle East, and Agora's cooking is reflective of that sweeping diversity. Many dishes incorporate Greek, Lebanese, and Middle Eastern flavors, illuminating Turkey's melting pot of cultures and culinary traditions.

Piece together a delectable ensemble by touring through Agora's rich tapestry of mezze. Start with a spread like baba ghanouj or labneh. Next, choose from lighter dishes like lentil soup, roasted beetroot salad, and grilled caulilini (baby cauliflower dressed in tahini, pomegranate, and olive oil). Cutting into a savory pideler, Turkey's famous flatbread,

Left: Mouthwatering mezze at Agora. *Top center:* Inside Agora's beautiful dining area. *Above center:* Dessert is served at Agora. *Right:* Agora's popular grilled octopus. Photos courtesy of Shab and Coop.

is a must here; choose from breads topped with Turkish meats and baked with cheeses. Relish delights like Agora's grilled octopus and ali nazik kebap, beef tenderloin cubes accompanied by smoked eggplant and yogurt. Groups can enjoy shareable platters of lamb shoulder and a whole fish served with grilled vegetables. End your culinary expedition on a sweet note, choosing from delectations like chocolate bavaroise and kunefe, shredded phyllo with sweet cheese and syrup served with Turkish rose ice cream and pistachios. To further immerse yourself, sip on raki, Turkey's national drink, made of twice-distilled grapes and aniseed that's traditionally served in a slender glass with chilled water and topped with ice.

1527 17th St. NW, 202-332-6767
7911 Westpark Dr., Tysons, VA, 703-663-8737
agorarestaurants.net

Visit Agora for daily lunch and dinner as well as bottomless brunch on the weekends. Happy hour occurs in their designated bar area Monday through Friday from 4 to 6:00 p.m.

HISTORIC HOTEL BARS OF WASHINGTON

Off the Record, Round Robin Bar, and the St. Regis Bar

From modest 18th-century boarding houses to opulent 19th-century establishments, sipping drinks at a historic hotel bar is a long-standing tradition that's helped define the culture of our nation's capital. Located just steps away from the White House, below are several legendary institutions that lie within the city's monumental core.

Off the Record may occupy the Hay-Adams's basement, but this sumptuous stalwart rises far above your typical watering hole. Known as DC's best "place to be seen and not heard," the dramatic speakeasy-esque hotel bar feels like a hideout for journalists, lobbyists, and the who's who of Washington's political and social scenes. The swanky haunt is characterized by its bold scarlet decor and walls adorned with political caricatures. A large, circular bar commands the space, and drinks are served on coasters displaying political caricatures ranging from President Obama to Florida Senator Marco Rubio. Off the Record boasts an impressive wine list and whips up masterful cocktails like their most popular drink, the Manhattan, as well as politically charged concoctions like the "Trumpy" Sour. Small plates like sliders and cheese plates will surely satisfy late-night cravings.

Mention a Washington historic hotel bar to most people and the Willard's Round Robin Bar will immediately come to mind. Established in 1847, the iconic bar has hosted a legion of prominent leaders, activists, and writers like President Woodrow Wilson, Mark Twain, and

Top center: Fall cocktails at Off the Record. Photo courtesy of the Hays-Adams Hotel. *Bottom center:* Round Robin Bar's mint julep. Photo courtesy of Willard InterContinental Washington, DC. *Right:* Off the Record's bold red interior. Photo courtesy of The Hays-Adams Hotel.

Walt Whitman. Sitting at its namesake circular bar is a quintessential experience in DC and somewhat of a rite of passage for those who call the area home. Don't miss its signature drink, the mint julep, which according to Willard legend was introduced here by Kentucky Senator Henry Clay to the DC area. In addition to the famed Southern favorite, the Round Robin offers whiskey-flight experiences highlighting several Ardbeg whiskey expressions. Food offerings include Maryland crab cakes, the Willard Burger, mussels, and steak frites.

Just a few blocks up the road stands the St. Regis, the 1926 landmark hotel that has hosted every president in office since its opening. The bar is imbued with history. Its back corner booth, named the General's Booth, pays tribute to General John J. Pershing, touted as only the second person after George Washington to be honored with the rank of "General of the Armies of the United States." Pershing was known to mix up old-fashioneds in his silver flask while seated in this booth.

Off the Record
Inside the Hay-Adams: 800 16th St. NW, 202-638-6600
hayadams.com/dining/off-the-record

Round Robin Bar
Inside the Willard Hotel: 1401 Pennsylvania Ave. NW, 202-628-9100
washington.intercontinental.com/food-drink/round-robin-bar

St. Regis Bar
Inside the St. Regis Hotel: 923 Black Lives Matter Plaza NW, 202-509-8000
marriott.com/en-us/hotels/wassx-the-st-regis-washington-dc/dining

Spiced roasted chicken with a side of
caramelized cauliflower at Chloe.
Photo courtesy of Scott Suchman.

RESTAURANTS A-Z

Many of the restaurants featured in this book have multiple locations in the DMV area; listed below are the main or original location(s). Plan your visit before you go!

2fifty BBQ
Multiple locations
4700 Riverdale Rd., Rivervale, MD

9292 Korean BBQ
7133 Little River Trnpk., unit A,
   Annandale, VA

A&J Restaurant
4316 Markham St., Annandale, VA
1319 Rockville Pike, Ste. C,
   Rockville, MD

Agora
1527 17th St. NW
7911 Westpark Dr., Tysons, VA

Albi
1346 4th St. SE

A. Litteri
517 Morse St. NE

Amazonia
920 Blagden Alley

Ambar
Multiple locations
523 8th St. SE

Amore Eats
1900 Rockville Pike, Rockville, MD

Anafre
3704 14th St. NW

Arcay Chocolates
1280 4th St. NE
3211 O St. NW

Arepa Zone
1121 14th St. NW

Astro Doughnuts
& Fried Chicken
Multiple locations
1308 G St. NW

Baked by Yæl
3000 Connecticut Ave. NW

Balangay
3607 Georgia Ave. NW

Bantam King
501 G St. NW

Beau Thai
1550 7th St. NW
3162 Mount Pleasant St. NW

Bee J's Cookies
beejscookies.com

Ben's Chili Bowl
Multiple locations
1213 U St. NW

Bob's Shanghai 66
305 N Washington St.,
   Rockville, MD

Breeze Bakery Cafe
4125 Hummer Rd., Annandale, VA

Bresca
1906 14th St. NW

Bronze
1245 H St. NE

Buffalo & Bergen
1309 5th St. NE
240 Massachusetts Ave. NE
3501 Connecticut Ave. NW

Call Your Mother Deli
Multiple locations
3301 Georgia Ave. NW

Cane
403 H St. NE

Capital City Mambo Sauce
capitalcity.com

Causa
920 Blagden Alley

Chaia
Multiple locations
3207 Grace St. NW

Chercher
3608 14th St. NW
4921 Bethesda Ave.,
    Bethesda, MD

Chloe
1331 4th St. SE

Compass Rose
1346 T St. NW

Daikaya
705 6th St. NW

DC Dosa
1731 Crystal Dr., Arlington, VA

Destiny's Pops
destinyspops.com

The District Fishwife
thedistrictfishwife.com

Dolcezza
Multiple locations
1704 Connecticut Ave. NW
dolcezzagelato.com

Don Juan Restaurant
1660 Lamont St. NW

Dukem
1114 U St. NW
1100 Maryland Ave.,
    Baltimore, MD

Eastern Market
225 7th St. SE

Eden Center
6751–6799 Wilson Blvd.,
    Falls Church, VA

Elcielo
1280 4th St. NE

Elfegne
2420 18th St. NW

Elizabeth's Gone Raw
1341 L St. NW

El Sol Restaurante & Tequileria
1227 11th St. NW
262 Cedar Ln., Ste. C, Vienna, VA

Ethiopic
401 H St. NE

Fava Pot
1817 M St. NW
7393 D Lee Hwy., Falls Church, VA

FishScale
637 Florida Ave. NW

Florida Avenue Grill
1100 Florida Ave. NW

Frankly . . . Pizza!
10417 Armory Ave.,
    Kensington, MD

Gloria's Pupuseria
3411 14th St. NW

Good Stuff Eatery
Multiple locations
303 Pennsylvania Ave. SE
goodstuffeatery.com

Haikan
805 V St. NW

HalfSmoke
Multiple locations
651 Florida Ave. NW

Hellbender Brewing Company
5788 2nd St. NE

Henry's Soul Cafe
1704 U St. NW
5431 Indianhead Hwy.,
    Oxen Hill, MD

Hitching Post Restaurant
200 Upshur St. NW

Honey Pig
Multiple locations
10045 Baltimore National Pike,
    Ellicott City, MD
honeypigbbq.com

Immigrant Food
Multiple locations
925 13th St. NW

Indigo
243 K St. NE

Joe's Noodle House
1488-C Rockville Pike,
    Rockville, MD

Jônt
1904 14th St. NW

José Andrés
joseandres.com/restaurants

KoChix
400 Florida Ave. NW

Kogiya
4220 Annandale Rd.,
    Annandale, VA

La Collina
747 C St. SE
lacollinadc.com

La Cosecha
1280 4th St. NE

Las Placitas
1100 8th St. SE

Laos in Town
250 K St. NE

Lapis
1847 Columbia Rd. NW

Last Call
1301-A 4th St. NE

L'Auberge Chez François
332 Springvale Rd.,
    Great Falls, VA

Lei Musubi
716 Monroe St. NE

Los Chorros
2420 Blueridge Ave.,
    Wheaton, MD

Love, Makoto
200 Massachusetts Ave. NW,
    Ste. 150

Magpie and the Tiger
magpieandthetiger.com

Makan
3400 11th St. NW

Manifest Bread
6208 Rhode Island Ave., Ste. 114,
    Riverdale Park, MD

Mariscos 1133
1133 11th St. NW

Martin's Tavern
1264 Wisconsin Ave. NW

Masseria
1340 4th St. NE

Maydān
1346 Florida Ave. NW

Méli Wine and Mezze
melidc.com

Mezcalero
3714 14th St. NW
8368 Richmond Hwy., Alexandria, VA

Mitsitam Native Foods Cafe
4th St. SW, Independence Ave. SW

Municipal Fish Market at the Wharf
1100 Maine Ave. SW

Nasime
1209 King St., Alexandria, VA

Nim Ali Shukos
clover.com/online-ordering/
nim-ali--washington

Off the Record
800 16th St. NW

Oohh's & Aahh's
5933 Georgia Ave. NW
1005 U St. NW

On Toast
ontoastdc.com

Open Crumb
1243 Good Hope Rd. SE

Our Mom Eugenia
Multiple locations
1025 Seneca Rd., Ste. H,
Great Valls, VA

Peruvian Brothers
4592 Eisenhower Ave.,
Alexandria, VA

Pie Shop
1339 H St. NE

Pineapple & Pearls
715 8th St. SE

Please Bring Chips
1320 H St. NE

Prescription Chicken
1819 7th St. NW

Puddin'
1309 5th St. NE

Queen's English
3410 11th St. NW

Republic Restoratives
1369 New York Ave. NW

Rice Paper
6775 Wilson Blvd., Falls Church, VA

Roaming Rooster
Multiple locations
3176 Bladensburg Rd. NE
roamingroosterdc.com

Round Robin Bar
1401 Pennsylvania Ave. NW

Rose's Luxury
717 8th St. SE

Samantha's Restaurant
631 University Blvd. E,
Silver Spring, MD

Santa Rosa Taqueria
santarosataqueria.com

Seylou Bakery & Mill
926 N St. NW

Shababi Palestinian Rotisserie Chicken
shababichicken.com

Sharbat
2473 18th St. NW

Sip and Sail DC
650 Wharf St. SW

Son of a Fish
sonofafishsushi.com

Stable
1324 H St. NE

Sticky Fingers Bakery & Diner
Multiple locations
406 H St. NE

St. James
2017 14th St. NW

St. Regis Bar
923 Black Lives Matter Plaza NW

Suburbia
1309 5th St. NE

Teaism
Multiple locations
400 8th St. NW

The Block Foodhall
4221 John Marr Dr., Annandale, VA
967 Rose Ave., North Bethesda, MD

The Duck & the Peach
300 7th St. SE

The Green Zone
2226 18th St. NW

The Wells
727 C St. SE

Timber Pizza Co.
809 Upshur St. NW

Tonari
707 6th St. NW

Union Market
1309 5th St. NE

Wagshal's
Multiple locations
4855 Massachusetts Ave. NW

Western Market
2000 Pennsylvania Ave. NW, #3500

We, The Pizza
Multiple locations
303 Pennsylvania Ave. SE

Wingo's
2218 Wisconsin Ave. NW

Xiquet
2404 Wisconsin Ave. NW

**Yekta Persian Market
& Kabob Counter**
1488 Rockville Pike, Rockville, MD

YELLOW
Multiple locations
1309 5th St. NE

Yum's II Carryout
1413 14th St. NW

Z&Z Manoushe Bakery
1111 Nelson St., Rockville, MD

APPENDIX

WASHINGTON, DC

ADAMS MORGAN

ANACOSTIA

CAPITOL HILL

COLUMBIA HEIGHTS

DOWNTOWN

DUPONT CIRCLE

EAST END

FEDERAL TRIANGLE

14TH STREET CORRIDOR

FOGGY BOTTOM